Reclaimed

AUTUMN 2013 COLLECTION

by Knit Picks

Printed in the United States of America

First Printing, 2013

ISBN 978-1-67267-010-4

Versa Press, Inc
800-447-7829

www.versapress.com

CONTENTS

Swarm of Bees, p22

Luxe, p98

Savitri, p34

Straight A, p62

Bellflower, p92

Callistoga, p52

Jayashri, p76

Gradual Scarf, p48

Addison, p16

Cable Embrace, p42

Atmos Cardigan, p68

Kyoko Toque and Mittens, p28

Belt Cardi, p82

Thick Chill, p58

Landslide Cowl, p10

LANDSLIDE COWL

by Kalurah Hudson

FINISHED MEASUREMENTS
30" Wide X 10" High with a 4" X 5" Tab (Unbuckled)

YARN
Knit Picks City Tweed HW (55% Merino Wool, 25% Superfine Alpaca, 20% Donegal Tweed (viscose neps); 164 yards/100g)
Orca 24537, 2 balls.

NEEDLES
US 10 (6mm) 24" or 32"circular needle, or size to obtain gauge for knitting back and forth.

NOTIONS
Yarn Needle
(2) Stitch Markers
Cable Needle
Repurposed Buckle Strap (Photo tutorial follows)

GAUGE
24 sts and 22 rows = 4" in Reversible Pebble Stitch pattern, blocked.
13 sts and 22 rows = 4" in Moss Stitch, blocked.

Landslide Cowl

Notes:

Landslide is an asymmetric cowl that can be worn several different ways, mimicking falling rocks down the side of a mossy hill.

It is knit in Moss Stitch and bordered with a pretty, reversible Pebble Stitch. The Pebble Stitch is a 1X1 Rib Cable pattern that creates an interesting, textured fabric.

Stitch markers are placed at the beginning and end of the Moss stitches so you don't lose your way.

The cowl is embellished with a repurposed buckle strap from an old pair of sandals. You could also cut up an old belt or a strap off of an old watch. (A handy step-by-step tutorial will help guide you.)

RRC – 1X1 Right Reversible Cable (worked over 4 stitches)
Slip first 2 stitches onto a cable needle, hold to back, K1, P1 over next 2 stitches, K1, P1 from cable needle.

LRC – 1X1 Left Reversible Cable (worked over 4 stitches)
Slip first 2 stitches onto a cable needle, hold to front, K1, P1 over next 2 stitches, K1, P1 from the cable needle.

Reversible Pebble Stitch (worked flat over 24 stitches)
WS Row 1: [K1, P1] 12 times.
Row 2 & 3: Rep. row 1.
Row 4: [RRC, LRC] 3 times.
Row 5-7: Rep. row 1.
Row 8: [LRC, RRC] 3 times.

Moss Stitch (worked flat over an even number of stitches)
WS Row 1: K1, P1.
Row 2: P1, K1.

DIRECTIONS
Cowl
CO 120 loosely, using long tail cast on.
WS Row 1: [K1, P1] across row.
Row 2: [K1, P1] 12 times, PM, [P1, K1] 36 times, PM, [K1, P1] 12 times.
Row 3: Rep. row 1, slipping all markers.
Row 4: [RRC, LRC] 3 times, SM, [P1, K1] 36 times, [RRC, LRC] 3 times.
Row 5: Rep. row 3.
Row 6: Rep. row 2.
Row 7: Rep. row 3.
Row 8: [LRC, RRC] 3 times, SM, [P1, K1] 36 times, [LRC, RRC] 3 times.
Row 9-48: Repeat rows 1-8 five more times. (a total of 40 more rows)
Row 49-55: Rep. rows 1-7.
RS Row 56: BO all 24 Pebble stitches, remove marker, BO in patt. all Moss stitches, remove marker, BO 1 more stitch, (you should now have 24 stitches left). Work row 8 of Pebble Stitch pattern over the 24 st that remain. (24 st)

Tab
WS Row 57-80: Work rows 1-8 of Pebble Stitch pattern three times (a total of 24 more rows).
Row 81: Rep. row 1 of Pebble Stitch pattern.
Row 82: Rep. row 2 of Pebble Stitch pattern.

BO all 24 stitches.

Finishing
Weave in ends, steam block and pin to diagram dimensions. When blocking piece, keep in mind the stitch per inch gauge of the Moss Stitch is very different from the Pebble Stitch gauge. You will want to block the Moss Stitch first then block the Pebble Stitch. Sew on your repurposed buckle. (See following tutorial guide)

Repurposed Buckle Tutorial
Using a strap with an attached buckle cut the strap off of your found item (such as a pair of old sandals or an old watch strap). I use a plastic ruler and a straight edge knife for this but if your leather is thin enough you can use a rotary cutter or a pair of sewing shears. If using a rotary cutter or straight edge knife, make sure to use a solid cutting surface such as a wood cutting board or thick quilting mat.

Be sure to cut the buckle end of the strap as well as the end with the holes. I keep the strap buckled before cutting to ensure that I'm allowing plenty of excess room on both sides of each strap for sewing onto the knit garment.

Mark your holes:

Using a ruler, mark on the leather using a very fine tip marker or white seamstress pencil where you want your holes to be. Judging on the width of the strap, I generally like to space each hole about 1/8" apart. Form a square shape with the holes. Repeat on other strap by placing the first strap on top of the second, using it as a template.

Punch holes:

Using a 1.8 mm size Leather Hole Punch (I purchased mine on Amazon.), punch a hole where you made each mark.

NOTE: You can use whatever size hole punch you like or you can use an awl tool. Just be sure the size you use coincides with the size of your sewing needle and that it will also accommodate the weight of yarn you will be sewing the straps on with.

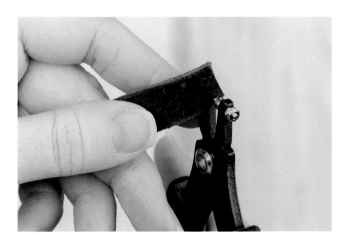
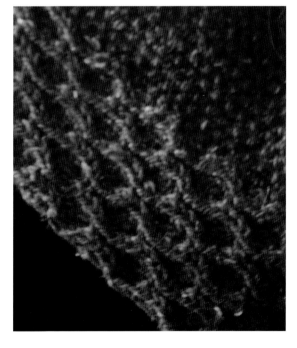

Sewing on Straps:

First, buckle up your strap. Fold up your neck warmer according to the photo, lay strap down over the folded tab and the neck warmer. Pin a marker to the edge of each end of the strap to serve as a guide when sewing them onto the neck warmer.

Thread your needle and using a Back Stitch, sew the strap onto the neck warmer. When you reach the first hole you started in, knot the ends of your yarn on the wrong side of the neck warmer and weave in the ends.

Repeat on other strap.

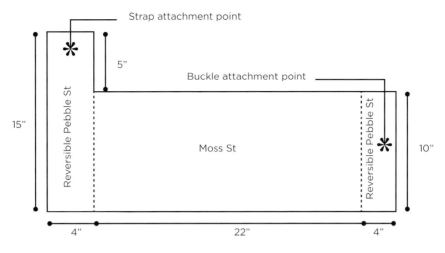

Strap attachment point

Reversible Pebble St

5"

Buckle attachment point

Reversible Pebble St

15"

Moss St

10"

4"   22"   4"

Abbreviations							
BO	bind off		and back of stitch	PU	pick up	SSP	sl, sl, p these 2 sts
cn	cable needle	K-wise	knitwise	P-wise	purlwise		tog tbl
CC	contrast color	LH	left hand	rep	repeat	SSSK	sl, sl, sl, k these 3 sts
CDD	Centered double	M	marker	Rev St st	reverse stockinette		tog
	dec	M1	make one stitch		stitch	St st	stockinette stitch
CO	cast on	M1L	make one left-lean-	RH	right hand	sts	stitch(es)
cont	continue		ing stitch	rnd(s)	round(s)	TBL	through back loop
dec	decrease(es)	M1R	make one right-	RS	right side	TFL	through front loop
DPN(s)	double pointed		leaning stitch	Sk	skip	tog	together
	needle(s)	MC	main color	Sk2p	sl 1, k2tog, pass	W&T	wrap & turn (see
EOR	every other row	P	purl		slipped stitch over		specific instructions
inc	increase	P2tog	purl 2 sts together		k2tog: 2 sts dec		in pattern)
K	knit	PM	place marker	SKP	sl, k, psso: 1 st dec	WE	work even
K2tog	knit two sts to-	PFB	purl into the front	SL	slip	WS	wrong side
	gether		and back of stitch	SM	slip marker	WYIB	with yarn in back
KFB	knit into the front	PSSO	pass slipped stitch	SSK	sl, sl, k these 2 sts	WYIF	with yarn in front
			over		tog	YO	yarn over

ADDISON

by Thayer Preece Parker

FINISHED MEASUREMENTS

30 (34.25, 38, 42.25, 46, 50.25, 54)" finished bust measurement; garment is meant to be worn with about 2" of negative ease.

YARN

Knit Picks Wool of the Andes Worsted (100% Peruvian Highland Wool; 110 yards/50g):
MC: Onyx Heather 24076, 10 (11, 13, 14, 15, 16, 17) balls;
CC: Marble Heather 25976, 2 (2, 2, 3, 3, 3, 3) balls.

NEEDLES

US 6 (4mm) circular needles, or size to obtain gauge
US 6 (4mm) DPNs or two 24" circular needles for two circulars technique, or one 32" or longer circular needle for Magic Loop technique, or size to obtain gauge
US 7 (4.5mm) circular needles, or size to obtain gauge
US 7 (4.5mm) DPNs or two 24" circular needles for two circulars technique, or one 32" or longer circular needle for Magic Loop technique, or size to obtain gauge

NOTIONS

Yarn Needle
Stitch Markers

GAUGE

17 sts and 23 rows = 4" in St st in the round, after blocking, using larger needle.

Addison

Notes:

Addison is worked from the hem up, in the round, with set-in sleeves. The collar and sleeves are also worked in the round, and depending on your preferred method, you may use DPNs, 2 circulars, or magic loop to knit those sections.

DIRECTIONS
Body
Hem

Using MC and smaller needle, CO 140 (158, 174, 192, 208, 226, 238) sts. PM for start of round, and join for working in the round. Begin working in 1x1 ribbing.

PM after 70 (79, 87, 96, 104, 113, 119) sts, then continue in ribbing until work measures 1 (1, 1, 1, 1.5, 1.5, 2, 2)" from CO edge. Switch to larger needle. K 4 rows in St st.

Stripes

Join CC and k 12 rounds.
Switch to MC and k 4 rounds.
Switch to CC and k 8 rounds.
Switch to MC and k 8 rounds.
Switch to CC and k 4 rounds.
Switch to MC and k 12 rounds.
Switch to CC and k 4 rounds.

The remainder of the body is knit using MC.

Join MC and continue working in St st until body measures 11 (10.75, 11.75, 11.25, 11.25, 12, 12.5)".

Decrease Round: *K1, K2tog, K until 3 st before marker, Ssk, K1, SM, repeat from *. 4 sts decreased.

Continuing in St st, repeat Decrease Round every 4 (4, 4, 4, 4, 5, 5) rows 7 (9, 9, 9, 9, 7, 6) more times. 108 (118, 134, 152, 168, 194, 210) sts.

Work evenly in St st until work measures 21.5 (22.5, 22.75, 22.5, 22.5, 22.75, 22.5)".

Increase Round: *K1, M1, K until 1 st before marker, M1, K1, repeat from *. 4 sts increased.

Continuing in St st, repeat Increase Round every 6 (4, 4, 4, 4, 4, 4) rows, 4 (6, 6, 6, 6, 4, 4) more times. 128 (146, 162, 180, 196, 214, 230) sts.

Work evenly in St st until work measures 29.5 (30.5, 31, 30.25, 30, 30.5, 30)".

Front

The front and back will now be separated and worked flat.

Row 1 (RS): BO 2 (3, 3, 4, 5, 5, 6) sts, k to next marker, turn. Remove marker and place remaining sts on stitch holder or waste yarn.
Row 2 (WS): BO 2 (3, 3, 4, 5, 5, 6) sts, P to end.
Row 3: BO 1 (2, 3, 3, 3, 4, 4) st(s), K to end.
Row 4: BO 1 (2, 3, 3, 3, 4, 4) st(s), P to end.
Row 5: K1, Ssk, K to end.

Row 6: P1, P2tog, P to end.

56 (61, 67, 74, 80, 87, 93) sts rem for front.

Continue in St st until piece measures 1.25 (1.5, 1.25, 1.25, 2, 2, 2.25)" from first underarm bind-off, ending with a RS row.

Next Row (WS): P 21 (22, 24, 26, 28, 30, 32), BO 14 (17, 19, 22, 24, 27, 29) sts, P to end.

Left Front

Row 1 (and all RS rows): K.
Row 2 (WS): BO 5 (5, 5, 6, 7, 8, 8) sts, P to end.
Row 4: BO 2 (2, 3, 3, 4, 4, 4) sts, P to end.
Row 6: BO 1 (2, 2, 2, 2, 2, 3) sts, P to end. 13 (13, 14, 15, 15, 16, 17) sts.

Continue working in St st until piece measures 5.5 (6, 6.25, 7, 7.25, 7.75, 8)" from first underarm bind-off, ending with a RS row.

Short Row 1 (WS): P 9 (9, 10, 10, 10, 11, 12), w&t.
Short Row 2: K to end.
Short Row 3: P 5 (5, 5, 5, 5, 6, 6), w&t.
Short Row 4: K to end.

BO purlwise across all shoulder sts, picking up and purling wraps together with the wrapped sts.

Right Front

With WS facing, join MC yarn at the outer edge.
Row 1 (and all WS rows): P.
Row 2 (RS): BO 5 (5, 5, 6, 7, 8, 8) sts, K to end.
Row 4: BO 2 (2, 3, 3, 4, 4, 4) sts, K to end.
Row 6: BO 1 (2, 2, 2, 2, 2, 3) sts, K to end. 13 (13, 14, 15, 15, 16, 17) sts rem.

Continue in St st until piece measures 5.5 (6, 6.25, 7, 7.25, 7.75, 8)" from first underarm bind-off, ending with a WS row.

Short Row 1 (RS): K 9 (9, 10, 10, 10, 11, 12), w&t.
Short Row 2: P to end.
Short Row 3: K 5 (5, 5, 5, 5, 6, 6), w&t.
Short Row 4: P to end.

BO knitwise across all shoulder sts, picking up and knitting wraps together with the wrapped stitches.

Back

Replace Back sts on needles. With RS facing, join MC at the right-hand edge.
Row 1 (RS): BO 2 (3, 3, 4, 5, 5, 6) sts, K to end.
Row 2 (WS): BO 2 (3, 3, 4, 5, 5, 6) st, P to end.
Row 3: BO 1 (2, 3, 3, 3, 4, 4) st(s), K to end.
Row 4: BO 1 (2, 3, 3, 3, 4, 4) st(s), P to end.
Row 5: K1, Ssk, K to end.
Row 6: P1, P2tog, P to end.

56 (61, 67, 74, 80, 87, 93) sts rem for back.

Continue in St st until piece measures 4.5 (5, 5.25, 6, 6.25, 6.75, 7)" from first underarm bind-off, ending with a WS row.

K 13 (13, 14, 15, 15, 16, 17), BO to last 13 (13, 14, 15, 15, 16, 17) sts, K to end.

Left Back

Work 5 rows in St st.

Short Row 1 (RS): K 9 (9, 10, 10, 10, 11, 12), w&t.

Short Row 2: P to end.

Short Row 3: K 5 (5, 5, 5, 5, 6, 6), w&t.

Short Row 4: P to end.

BO knitwise across all shoulder st, picking up and knitting wraps together with the wrapped sts.

Right Back

With RS facing, join MC yarn at right hand side of live stitches. Work 5 rows in St st.

Short Row 1 (WS): P 9 (9, 10, 10, 10, 11, 12), w&t.

Short Row 2: K to end.

Short Row 3: P 5 (5, 5, 5, 5, 6, 6), w&t.

Short Row 4: K to end.

BO purlwise across all shoulder st, picking up and purling wraps together with the wrapped sts.

Seaming and Collar

Turn the work inside-out and hold the front and back shoulder pieces together with WS facing out. With a yarn needle, seam shoulder stitches together. Turn the work right-side out again.

With smaller size DPNs or circular needles, starting at the center back neck, pick up an even number of sts around the neckline, 1 st for every BO st along the back and front, and 3 sts for every 4 rows along the sides. Work in 1x1 ribbing for 1". BO all sts.

Sleeves

With larger DPNs or circular needles, beginning at center of underarm, pick up and knit 48 (52, 56, 60, 64, 68, 74) sts around the arm hole, placing a marker halfway, at the top of the shoulder—1 st for every underarm BO st, and about 1 st for every 2 rows along the sides. If there are a few extra stitches, decrease

those at the center underarm after the short row section to achieve the desired number of sleeve sts. PM for start of the row.

Short Rows:

Row 1: K to 4 sts past the shoulder marker, w&t.

Row 2: P to 4 sts past the shoulder marker, w&t.

Row 3: K to 5 sts past the shoulder marker, w&t.

Row 4: P to 5 sts past the shoulder marker, w&t.

Continue in this manner, wrapping one st past the previous wrap on each row. Do not pick up the wraps. Continue until all sts except the underarm sts have been wrapped. On the final RS row, K until the underarm marker. Remove shoulder marker on the next round.

Work in St st in the round until sleeve measures 3.25 (3.25, 4.25, 4, 4, 4.5, 4.5)" from underarm.

Decrease Round: K1, K2tog, K to 3 st before M, Ssk, K1.

Continuing in St st, work Decrease Round every 15 (10, 9, 7, 7, 6, 4) rows 2 (3, 3, 4, 4, 4, 6) more times. 42 (44, 48, 50, 54, 58, 60) sts rem.

If necessary, work evenly in St st until piece measures 8.75 (8.75, 9, 9, 9, 8.75, 8.75)" from underarm.

Join CC and K 4 rows.

Switch to MC and K 4 rows.

Switch to CC and K 8 rows.

Switch to CC. With smaller DPNs or circular needles, work in 1x1 ribbing for 1 (1, 1, 1.5, 1.5, 2, 2)". BO all sts.

Work second sleeve identical to first.

Finishing

Weave in ends, taking care around the color joins to ensure that any holes in the fabric are pulled tight and closed. Wash and block to diagram or desired measurements.

Abbreviations		PM	Place marker
BO	Bind off	P2tog	Purl 2 sts together
CC	Contrast color	rem	Remaining
CO	Cast on	RS	Right side
K	Knit	SM	Slip marker
K2tog	Knit 2 sts together	st(s)	Stitch(es)
M1	Make 1 stitch	St st	Stockinette stitch
MC	Main color	WS	Wrong Side
P	Purl	w&t	Wrap and turn

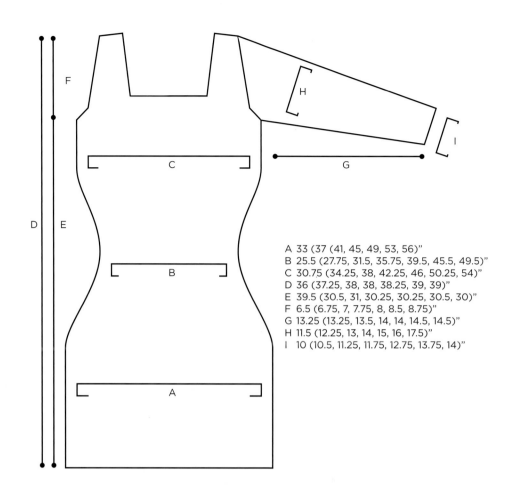

A 33 (37 (41, 45, 49, 53, 56)"
B 25.5 (27.75, 31.5, 35.75, 39.5, 45.5, 49.5)"
C 30.75 (34.25, 38, 42.25, 46, 50.25, 54)"
D 36 (37.25, 38, 38, 38.25, 39, 39)"
E 39.5 (30.5, 31, 30.25, 30.25, 30.5, 30)"
F 6.5 (6.75, 7, 7.75, 8, 8.5, 8.75)"
G 13.25 (13.25, 13.5, 14, 14, 14.5, 14.5)"
H 11.5 (12.25, 13, 14, 15, 16, 17.5)"
I 10 (10.5, 11.25, 11.75, 12.75, 13.75, 14)"

SWARM OF BEES

by Lisa Kereliuk

FINISHED MEASUREMENTS

30 (34, 38, 42, 46, 50)" finished bust measurement; garment is meant to be worn with 2 to 6" of negative ease. Choose a size smaller than your bust measurement.

YARN

Knit Picks Capra (85% Merino, 15% Cashmere; 123 yards/50g):
Turmeric 25950, 7 (8, 8, 9, 10, 11) balls

NEEDLES

US 4 (3.5mm) circular needles, or size to obtain gauge
US 6 (4mm) circular needles, or size to obtain gauge
US 4 (3.5mm) DPNs or extra circular needle for two circulars technique, or one 32" or longer circular needle for Magic Loop technique, or size to obtain gauge

NOTIONS

Yarn Needle
Stitch Markers
Scrap yarn

GAUGE

25 sts and 26 rounds = 4" over honeycomb pattern on 4mm needles, blocked.
20 sts and 34 rounds = 4" over bee swarm pattern on 4mm needles, blocked.
18 sts and 40 rounds = 4" over bee stitch pattern on 4mm needles, blocked.

Swarm of Bees

Notes:

This sweater is worked from the top down starting from the side of the neck. It is shaped by changing the stitch pattern and stitch count in each segment, bridging the transition by using gradually larger or smaller needles. Because of the limited depth of shaping throughout the yoke, the sweater will fit best when knit with significant negative ease. A sweater knit with more negative ease will require a longer length from yoke to underarm to account for the stretch across the bust, and a sweater knit with less negative ease will require a shorter length from yoke to underarm. Over the bee stitch at the hip, a mock seam is added at the opposite side to mirror the look of the start and end of round.

Honeycomb Stitch Pattern (worked in the round over a multiple of 4 (increased to 6) stitches)

Round 1: *K1, M1R, K3, M1L, repeat from * to end of round
Rounds 2, 3, 4, and 5: *K3, P1, K2, repeat from * to end of round
Round 6: *K1, K2tog, K1, SSK, repeat from * to end of round
Round 7: *K2, M1L, K1, M1R, K1, repeat from * to end of round
Rounds 8, 9, 10, and 11: *P1, K5, repeat from * to end of round
Round 12: *K1, SSK, K1, K2tog, repeat from * to end of round

Also see chart

Bee Swarm Stitch Pattern (worked in the round over an even number of stitches)

See Chart

Bee Stitch (worked in the round between markers)

Round 1: Purl
Round 2: *K1, [K1below, K1] to one stitch before marker, K1, slip marker, repeat from * to end of round
Round 3: Purl
Round 4: *K1, [K1, K1below] to one stitch before marker, K1, slip marker, repeat from * to end of round

Also see chart

DIRECTIONS
Body

Neck

With US 4 (3.5mm) double pointed needles, cast on 116 (120, 132, 144, 152, 160) stitches and join to work in the round.

Rounds 1, 2, and 3: Purl
Round 4 and 5: Knit
Round 6: *K3, KFB, repeat from * to end of round.

145 (150, 165, 180, 190, 200) stitches

When neckline is wide enough, switch to US 4 (3.5mm) circular needles, and place marker at beginning of round.

Rounds 7, 8, and 9: Purl
Round 10 and 11: Knit
Round 12: *K4, KFB, repeat from * to end of round.

174 (180, 198, 216, 228, 240) stitches

SIZE 38 ONLY
Next 3 Rounds: Purl
Next 2 Rounds: Knit
Next Round: *K18, KFB, [K19, KFB] four times, repeat from * to end of round.

208 stitches

SIZE 42 ONLY
Next 3 Rounds: Purl
Next 2 Rounds: Knit
Next Round: *[K11, KFB] 8 times, K12, repeat from * to end of round.

232 stitches

SIZE 46 ONLY
Next 3 Rounds: Purl
Next 2 Rounds: Knit
Next Round: *K11, KFB, [K23, KFB] four times, repeat from * to last 12 stitches, K11, KFB.

239 stitches

SIZE 50 ONLY
Next 3 Rounds: Purl
Next 2 Rounds: Knit
Next Round: *K11, KFB, repeat from * to end of round

260 stitches

ALL SIZES
Next 2 Rounds: Purl
Next Round: Purl across the round, increasing 2 (4, 0, 0, 1, 4) stitches evenly around using PFB.

176 (184, 208, 232, 240, 264) stitches

Yoke

Begin honeycomb chart. Work two repeats (24 rounds) of honeycomb pattern stitch. Switch to larger needles. Work in pattern until piece measures approximately 6 (6.5, 7, 7.5, 8, 8.25) inches, ending on any row except row 5, 6, 11 or 12.

264 (276, 312, 348, 360, 396) stitches

Divide for Arms

Cast on 12 (18, 18, 18, 24, 24) stitches at end of round. Slide the next 48 (48, 54, 60, 60, 66) stitches onto waste yarn for first sleeve.

Work in honeycomb stitch pattern across 84 (90, 102, 114, 120, 132) stitches for back. Slip the next 48 (48, 54, 60, 60, 66) stitches onto waste yarn for the second sleeve.

Cast on 12 (18, 18, 18, 24, 24) stitches. Work across the next 84 (90, 102, 114, 120, 132) stitches on the circular needles in honeycomb stitch pattern for the front. Slip next 6 (9, 9, 9, 12, 12) stitches, carrying working yarn across the back for stitches that would have been knit and carrying yarn across the front for stitches that would have been purled.

192 (216, 240, 264, 288, 312) stitches.

Place marker to indicate new beginning of round.

Bust

Continue to work in honeycomb pattern, slipping marker as you come to it. Work 30 rounds with the larger needles, then switch to smaller needles and continue to work in honeycomb pattern until work measures 8.5 inches from armhole, ending on round 6 or 12.

Belt detail looks best when it falls around the narrowest part of the body. Try on the sweater as you go for correct placement. If you have an unusually short waist or are working the pattern with less than 4 inches of negative ease, you may want to work fewer chart repeats. If you have an unusually long waist or you are working the pattern with more than 4 inches of negative ease, you may want to work more.

128 (144, 160, 176, 192, 208) stitches

Waist

Setup:

SIZE 30 – *K1, K2tog, [K18, K2tog] three times, K1, place marker, repeat from * to end of round.

SIZE 34 – *K1, K2tog, K66, K2tog, K1, place marker, repeat from * to end of round.

SIZE 38 – K around, placing marker after 80 stitches.

SIZE 42 – *K1, KFB, K83, KFB, K2, place marker, repeat from * to end of round

SIZE 46 – *K1, KFB, [K29, KFB] twice, K31 KFB, K2, place marker, repeat from * to end of round.

SIZE 50 – *K1, KFB, [K19, KFB] five times, K2, place marker, repeat from * to end of round.

120 (140, 160, 180, 200, 220) stitches.

Switch to larger needles. Work bee swarm chart (multiple of 20 stitches) for 22 rounds.

Hip

Setup:

SIZE 30 - *[K5, KFB] 9 times, K6, repeat from * to end of round.

SIZE 34 - *[K6, KFB] 9 times, K7, repeat from * to end of round.

SIZE 38 - *[K9, KFB] 7 times, K10, repeat from * to end of round.

SIZE 42 - *K9, KFB, repeat from * to end of round.

SIZE 46 - *K19, KFB, repeat from * to end of round.

SIZE 50 - *K19, KFB, repeat from * to last 20 stitches, K20.

138 (158, 174, 198, 210, 230) stitches.

ALL SIZES

Work in bee stitch pattern for approximately 2.75 (3, 3.25, 3.5, 3.75, 3.75) inches, or until approximately 1 inch shorter than desired length.

Garter Hem

Round 1: K3 (5, 3, 0, 3, 5), *K8, KFB, repeat from * to end.

150 (175, 193, 220, 233, 255) stitches.

Next 2 rounds: Purl
Next 2 rounds: Knit
Next 2 rounds: Purl

Bind off loosely knitwise.

Sleeves

Slide the stitches from waste yarn onto circular needle or dpns. Attach your working yarn and use it to pick up 12 (18, 18, 18, 24, 24) stitches from underarm cast on. Join to knit in the round.

60 (66, 72, 78, 84, 90) stitches.

Round 1: Knit
Next 2 rounds: Purl
Next 2 rounds: Knit
Next 2 rounds: Purl

Bind off loosely knitwise.

Repeat for the second sleeve.

Finishing

Weave in ends, wash and block to diagram.

Bee Stitch Chart (worked in the round between markers)

4	3	2	1	
	↓			4
●	●	●	●	3
		↓		2
●	●	●	●	1

Honeycomb Chart (worked in the round over a multiple of 4 (increased to 6)

6	5	4	3	2	1	
▓		╱		╲	▓	12
					●	11
					●	10
					●	9
					●	8
	MR		ML			7
	╲	▓		▓	╱	6
		●				5
		●				4
		●				3
		●				2
ML			MR			1

Legend:

●	**purl**	purl stitch
□	**knit**	knit stitch
V	**slip**	Slip stitch as if to purl, holding yarn in back

Right Twist
Skip the first stitch, knit into 2nd stitch, then knit skipped stitch. Slip both stitches from needle together OR k2tog leaving sts on LH needle, then k first st again, sl both sts off needle.

Left Twist
sl1 to CN, hold in front. k1, k1 from CN

make one right
Place a firm backward loop over the right needle, so that the yarn end goes towards the back

make one left
Place a firm backward loop over the right needle, so that the yarn end goes towards the front

k2tog
Knit two stitches together as one stitch

No Stitch
Placeholder - No stitch made.

ssk
Slip one stitch as if to knit, Slip another stitch as if to knit. Insert left-hand needle into front of these 2 stitches and knit them together

k in st below
Knit into stitch below, inserting needle from front through the st in the row below

Bee Swarm Chart (worked in the round over an even number of stitches)

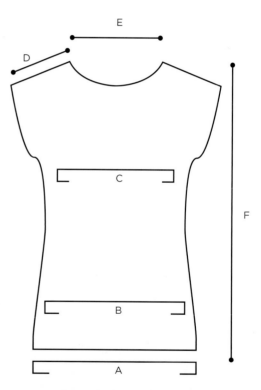

A 32 (36, 40, 44, 48, 52)"
B 30.6 (35.1, 38.6, 46.7, 51.1)"
C 30 (34, 38, 42, 46, 50)"
D 6 (6.5, 7, 7.5, 8, 8.3)"
E 9.8 (10, 11, 12, 12.5, 13.5)"
F 22.3 (23, 23.8, 24.5, 25.5)"

KYOKO TOQUE & FINGERLESS MITTENS

by Megan Grewal

FINISHED MEASUREMENTS

Toque:
19.25 (20.5, 22)" finished circumference
8 (8.5, 9.25)" finished height
Toque is meant to be worn with approximately 2" of negative ease.

Fingerless Mitts:
7.5 (8, 9)" finished hand circumference
5.5 (6.5, 7.5)" wrist-to-fingertip length
Fingerless Mitts is meant to be worn with 0" ease

YARN

Knit Picks Capretta (80% Fine Merino Wool, 10% Cashmere, 10% Nylon; 230 yards/50g): Topaz 25944, 2 balls (1 ball each for the toque and mitts)

NEEDLES

US 3 (3.25mm) 24-32" or longer circular needle for Magic Loop technique, or size to obtain gauge
US 2 (3mm) 16" long circular needles, or 2 sizes smaller than size needed to obtain gauge

NOTIONS

Yarn Needle
8 Stitch Markers
Cable Needle
Waste Yarn

GAUGE

25 sts and 36 rows = 4" x 4" in St st in the round, blocked.
26 sts and 36 rows = 3.25" wide x 2.75" high in Cable Pattern, blocked.

Kyoko Toque & Fingerless Mittens

Notes:

Toque is begun with Judy's Magic Cast On and worked from the top down, seamlessly in the round. Fingerless mitts are worked from the cuff up, seamlessly in the round. Both pieces feature a charted & written cable pattern, on a reverse stockinette background, with stockinette side panels on the toque and on the palm of the mitts. Twisted rib is worked along the cuffs and brim of the toque. Rounds 1-24 are repeated for the Cable Chart.

Judy's Magic Cast On:
www.knitpicks.com/wptutorials/Judys-Magic-Cast-On

Magic Loop Method:
www.knitpicks.com/wptutorials/magic-loop

Special Stitches:

2/1LPC - 2/1 left purl cable: Sl 2sts onto cable needle, hold in front, p1, k2 tbl from cable needle.

2/1RPC - 2/1 right purl cable: Sl 1st onto cable needle, hold in back; k2 tbl, p1 from cable needle.

2/2LC - 2/1 left cross cable: Sl 2sts onto cable needle, hold in front; k2 tbl, k2 tbl from cable needle.

2/2RC - 2/2 right cross cable: Sl 2sts onto cable needle, hold in back; k2 tbl, k2 tbl from cable needle.

LLI - make 1 left: Insert left hand needle into the second leg of the previous st; k through the leg.

RLI - make 1 right: Insert right hand needle into the first leg of the following st; k through the leg.

Pfb - purl front & back: P into the front and the back of the following st.

Cable Pattern (worked in the round over 26 sts & 24 rounds)
Note: All knit sts are worked through the back loops.
Round 1: (K2 tbl, p3) x2, k2 tbl, p2, k2 tbl, (p3, k2 tbl) x2.
All Even-numbered Rounds: K tbl the k sts and p the p sts.
Round 3: (2/1LPC, p2) x2, 2/1LPC, 2/1RPC, (p2, 2/1RPC) x2.
Round 5: P1, (2/1LPC, p2) x2, 2/2LC, (p2, 2/1RPC) x2, p1.
Round 7: (P2, 2/1LPC) x2, 2/1RPC, 2/1LPC, (2/1RPC, p2) x2.
Round 9: P3, 2/1LPC, p2, (2/2RC, p2) x2, 2/1RPC, p3.
Round 11: P4, (2/1LPC, 2/1RPC) x3, p4.
Round 13: P5, (2/2LC, p2) x3, p3.
Round 15: P4, (2/1RPC, 2/1LPC) x3, p4.
Round 17: P3, 2/1RPC, (p2, 2/2RC) x2, p2, 2/1LPC, p3.
Round 19: (P2, 2/1RPC) x2, 2/1LPC, 2/1RPC, (2/1LPC, p2) x2.
Round 21: P1, (2/1RPC, p2) x2, 2/2LC, (p2, 2/1LPC) x2, p1.
Round 23: (2/1RPC, p2) x2, 2/1RPC, 2/1LPC, (p2, 2/1LPC) x2.

Twisted Rib 2x2 Pattern (worked in the round, over a multiple of 4 sts)
All Rounds: (K2 tbl, p2) to end.

Twisted Rib 1x1 Pattern (worked in the round, over a multiple of 2 sts)

All Rounds: (K1 tbl, p1) to end.

DIRECTIONS
Toque

Toque is worked from the crown to the brim, in the round.

Crown - Top of Toque Shaping

Using larger size needles with the Magic Loop Method, use Judy's Magic Cast On and CO 60 sts, 30 sts onto each needle.

Beg working in the round, increasing and working from Round 1 of Cable Chart, as follows:

Round 1 (set up for cables & ear flaps, increases every 2nd round): K1, PM for beg of round, *p1, PM, work Round 1 of Chart, PM, p1, PM, kfb x2, PM*; rep from * to * once more. 64 sts
Round 2: *P1, SM, work Round 2 of Chart, SM, p1, SM, k4, SM*; rep from * to * once more.

Note: Cont working consecutive rounds of Cable Chart between stitch markers as established:

Round 3: *P1, SM, work Round 3 of Chart, SM, p1, SM, k1, M1R, k2, M1L, k1, SM*; rep from * to * once more. 68 sts
Round 4: *P1, SM, work Round 4 of Chart, SM, p1, SM, k6, SM*; rep from * to * once more.
Round 5: *P1, SM, work Round 5 of Chart, SM, p1, SM, k1, M1R, k4, M1L, k1, SM*; rep from * to * once more. 72 sts
Round 6: *P1, SM, work Round 6 of Chart, SM, p1, SM, k8, SM*; rep from * to * once more.
Round 7: *P1, SM, work Round 7 of Chart, SM, p1, SM, k1, M1R, k6, M1L, k1, SM*; rep from * to * once more. 76 sts
Round 8: *P1, SM, work Round 8 of Chart, SM, p1, SM, k10, SM*; rep from * to * once more.
Round 9: *P1, SM, work Round 9 of Chart, SM, p1, SM, k1, M1R, k8, M1L, k1, SM*; rep from * to * once more. 80 sts
Round 10: *P1, SM, work Round 9 of Chart, SM, p1, SM, k12, SM*; rep from * to * once more.
Round 11 (front & back increases beg, every 2nd rnd): *Pfb, SM, Round 11 of Chart, SM, pfb, SM, k1, M1R, k10, M1L, k1 SM*; rep from * to * once more. 88 sts
Round 12: *P2, SM, work Round 12 of Chart, SM, p2, SM, k14, SM*; rep from * to * once more.
Round 13: *Pfb, p1, SM, work Round 13 of Chart, SM, p1, pfb, SM, k1, M1R, k12, M1L, k1, SM*; rep from * to * once more. 96 sts
Round 14: *P3, SM, work Round 14 of Chart, SM, k16, SM*; rep from * to * once more.
Round 15: *Pfb, p2, SM, work Round 15 of Chart, SM, p2, pfb, SM, k1, M1R, k14, M1R, k1, SM*; rep from * to * once more. 104 sts
Round 16: *P4, SM, work Round 16 of Chart, SM, p4, SM, k18, SM*; rep from * to * once more.
Round 17: *Pfb, p3, SM, work Round 17 of Chart, SM, p3, pfb, SM, k1, M1R, k16, M1L, k1, SM*; rep from * to * once more. 112 sts
Round 18: *P5, SM, work Round 18 of Chart, SM, p5, SM, k20, SM*; rep from * to * once more.
Round 19: *Pfb, p4, SM, work Round 19 of Chart, SM, p4, pfb, SM, k1, M1R, k18, M1L, k1, SM*; rep from * to * once more. 120 sts

Round 20: *P6, SM, work Round 20 of Chart, SM, p6, SM, k22, SM*; rep from * to * once more.

Round 21 (earflap increases only, EVERY rnd): *P6, remove marker, work Round 21 of Chart, remove marker, p6, SM, k1, M1R, k20, M1L, k1, SM*; rep from * to * once more. 124 sts

Round 22: *P6, work Round 22 of Chart, p6, SM, k1, M1R, k22, M1L, k1, SM*; rep from * to * once more. 128 sts

Round 23: *P6, work Round 23 of Chart, p6, SM, k1, M1R, k24, M1L, k1, SM*; rep from * to * once more. 132 sts

Sizes Medium & Large ONLY:

Round 24: *P6, work Round 24 of Chart, p6, p6, SM, k1, M1R, k26, M1L, k1, SM*; rep from * to * once more. 136 sts

Round 25: *P6, work Round 1 of Chart, p6, p6, k1, M1R, k28, M1L, k1, SM*; rep from * to * once more. 140 sts

Size Large ONLY:

Round 26: *P6, work Round 2 of Chart, p6 , p6, k1, M1R, k30, M1L, k1, SM*; rep from * to * once more. 144 sts

Round 27: *P6, work Round 3 of Chart, p6, p6, SM, k1, M1R, k32, M1L, k1, SM*; rep from * to * once more. 148 sts

All Sizes Cont:
Body of Toque

Next Round: *P6, work Round 24 (2, 4) of Chart, p6, SM, k to marker, SM*; rep from * to * once.

Cont working consecutive rounds of chart as established, without increasing, until toque measures 6.5 (7, 7.5)" or 1.5" less than final length, removing markers (except for beg of round marker) on last round.

Brim

Next Round: Work in Twisted Rib 2x2 and dec 8sts evenly across the front Cable Chart and 8 sts evenly across the back Cable chart. 116 (124, 132) sts

Cont in Twisted Rib 2x2 for 1.5", then BO all sts loosely in 2x2 rib (do NOT twist sts).

Fingerless Mitts
Cuff

With smaller size needles, loosely CO 40 (48, 52) sts; join to work in the round, being careful not to twist sts, and PM for beg of round. Work in Twisted Rib 2x2 for 2.75 (3, 3.25)".

RIGHT HAND

Switch to larger needles and set up for Cable Chart, as follows:

Size Small: K1 tbl, p1, PM, pfb, p1, k2 tbl, pfb, p1, RLI, k2 tbl, LLI, p2, RLI, k2 tbl, LLI, p1, pfb, k2 tbl, p1, pfb, PM, p1, k1 tbl, PM, k2, PM, k to end of round. 48 sts

Size Medium: K1 tbl, p2, PM, p1, (k2 tbl, pfb, p1) x2, RLI, k2 tbl, LLI, (p1, pfb, k2 tbl) x2, p1, PM, p2, k1 tbl, PM, k2, PM, k to end of round. 54 sts

Size Large: K1 tbl, p3, PM, pfb, p3, (RLI, k2 tbl, LLI, p2) x2, RLI, k2 tbl, LLI, p3, pfb, PM, p3, k1 tbl, PM, k2, PM, k to end of round. 60 sts

All Sizes:

Next Round: K1 tbl, p1 (2, 3), SM, work Round 8 (22, 14) of Chart, SM, p1 (2, 3), k1 tbl, SM, k to end of round, slipping all markers. Rep last round 4 (6, 8) more times, working consecutive rounds

of cable Chart.

Thumb Gusset

Round 1: K1 tbl, p1 (2, 3), SM, work Round 13 (5, 23) of Chart, SM, p 1 (2, 3), k1 tbl, SM, RLI, k to marker, LLI, SM, k to end of round. 50 (56, 62) sts

Round 2: K1 tbl, p1 (2, 3), SM, work Round 14 (6, 24) of Chart, SM, p 1 (2, 3), k1 tbl, SM, k to marker, SM, k to end of round. Rep last 2 rounds 6 (7, 8) more times, working consecutive rounds of cable Chart.

62 (70, 78) sts

Hand

Next Round (remove thumb sts): K1 tbl, p1 (2, 3), SM, work Round 3 (21, 17) of Chart, SM, p 1 (2, 3), k1 tbl, SM, place following 16 (18, 20) sts onto waste yarn, remove marker, CO 4sts, k to end of round. 50 (56, 62) sts

Cable Round: K1 tbl, p1 (2, 3), SM, work Round 4 (22, 18) of Chart,, SM, p 1 (2, 3), k1 tbl, SM, k to end of round.

Cont repeating cable round, working consecutive rounds of cable Chart, until mitten measures 4.5 (5.5, 6.5)" from beg of cable Chart. End after round 24 of Cable Chart.

Switch to smaller needles and set up for rib as follows:

Beg working in Twisted Rib 2x2 and dec 6 (4, 6) sts over the first 30 (32, 34) sts. 44 (52, 56) sts

Cont in Twisted Rib 2x2 for 1". BO all sts loosely.

Thumb

With larger size needles, beg at center of thumb gusset, pick up and k 2sts, k all sts on needle, pick up and k 2 sts at gusset, PM for beg of rnd. 20 (22, 24) sts

Next Round: K1, k2tog, k to last 3sts, ssk, k1. 18 (20, 22) sts
Next Round: K2tog, k to last 2sts, ssk. 16 (18, 20) sts

K 2 rounds.
Beg Twisted Rib 1x1 and work for .75".
BO all sts in 1x1 rib (do NOT twist sts).

LEFT HAND
Cuff

With smaller size needles, loosely CO 40 (48, 52) sts; join to work in the round, being careful not to twist sts, and PM for beg of round. Beg with p2 and work in Twisted Rib 2x2 for 2.75 (3, 3.25)".

Switch to larger needles and set up for Cable Chart, as follows:

Size Small: K16, PM, k2, PM, k1 tbl, p1, PM, pfb, p1, k2tbl, pfb, p1, RLI, k2 tbl, LLI, p2, RLI, k2 tbl, LLI, p1, pfb, k2 tbl, p1, pfb, PM, p1, k1 tbl. 48 sts

Size Medium: K20, PM, k2, PM, k1 tbl, p2, PM, p1, (k2 tbl, pfb, p1) x2, RLI, k2 tbl, LLI, (p1, pfb, k2 tbl) x2, p1, PM, p2, k1 tbl. 54 sts

Size Large: K24, PM, k2, PM, k1 tbl, p3, PM, pfb, p3, (RLI, k2 tbl, LLI, p2) x2, RLI, k2 tbl, LLI, p3, pfb, PM, p3, k1 tbl. 60 sts

All Sizes:

Next Round: K to marker, SM, k2, SM, k1 tbl, p1 (2, 3), SM, work

Round 8 (22, 14) of Chart, SM, p1 (2, 3), k1 tbl.
Rep last round 4 (6, 8) more times, working consecutive rounds of cable Chart.

Thumb Gusset

Round 1: K to marker, SM, RLI, k to marker, LLI, SM, k1 tbl, p1 (2, 3), SM, work Round 13 (5, 23) of Chart, SM, p 1 (2, 3), k1 tbl. 50 (56, 62)sts
Round 2: (K to marker, sm) x2, k1 tbl, p1 (2, 3), SM, work Round 14 (6, 24) of Chart, SM, p 1 (2, 3), k1 tbl.
Rep last 2 rounds 6 (7, 8) more times, working consecutive rounds of cable Chart.

62 (70, 78) sts

Hand

Next Round (remove thumb sts): K to marker, remove marker,
place following 16 (18, 20) sts onto waste yarn, CO 4sts, SM, k1 tbl, p1 (2, 3), SM, work Round 3 (21, 17) of Chart, SM, p 1 (2, 3), k1 tbl. 50 (56, 62)sts

Cable Round: K to marker, SM, k1 tbl, p1 (2, 3), SM, work Round 4 (22, 18) of Chart, SM, p 1 (2, 3), k1 tbl.

Cont repeating cable round, working consecutive rounds of cable Chart, until mitten measures 4.5 (5.5, 6.5)" from beg of cable Chart. End after round 24 of Cable Chart.

Switch to smaller needles and set up for rib as follows:
Beg working in Twisted Rib 2x2 and dec 6 (4, 6) sts over the first 30 (32, 34) sts. 44 (52, 56) sts
Cont in Twisted Rib 2x2 for 1". BO all sts loosely.

Thumb

Work as for Right Hand.

Finishing

Weave in ends, wash and block to final measurements.

Abbreviations								
BO	bind off	K-wise	knitwise	PU	pick up	SSP	sl, sl, p these 2 sts tog tbl
cn	cable needle	LH	left hand	P-wise	purlwise		
CC	contrast color	M	marker	rep	repeat	SSSK	sl, sl, sl, k these 3 sts tog
CDD	Centered double dec	M1	make one stitch	Rev St st	reverse stockinette stitch	St st	stockinette stitch
CO	cast on	M1L	make one left-leaning stitch	RH	right hand	sts	stitch(es)
cont	continue	M1R	make one right-leaning stitch	rnd(s)	round(s)	TBL	through back loop
dec	decrease(es)			RS	right side	TFL	through front loop
DPN(s)	double pointed needle(s)	MC	main color	Sk	skip	tog	together
		P	purl	Sk2p	sl 1, k2tog, pass slipped stitch over k2tog: 2 sts dec	W&T	wrap & turn (see specific instructions in pattern)
EOR	every other row	P2tog	purl 2 sts together				
inc	increase	PM	place marker	SKP	sl, k, psso: 1 st dec	WE	work even
K	knit	PFB	purl into the front and back of stitch	SL	slip	WS	wrong side
K2tog	knit two sts together			SM	slip marker	WYIB	with yarn in back
		PSSO	pass slipped stitch over	SSK	sl, sl, k these 2 sts tog	WYIF	with yarn in front
KFB	knit into the front and back of stitch					YO	yarn over

SAVITRI

by Meghan Jones

FINISHED MEASUREMENTS

34 (38, 42, 46, 50, 54, 58, 62)" finished bust measurement; garment is meant to be worn with 2" positive ease.

YARN

Knit Picks Wool of the Andes Bulky (100% Peruvian Highland Wool; 137 yards/100g):
Masala 24681, 8 (9, 10, 11, 12, 13, 14, 15) skeins.

NEEDLES

US 10 (6mm) 36" circular needles, or size to obtain gauge

NOTIONS

Yarn Needle
Stitch Markers
Cable needles
Scrap yarn or stitch holder
Nine 1 5/8" buttons
Optional sewn-on snap

GAUGE

14 sts and 20 rows = 4" in St st, blocked.
14 sts and 20 rows = 4" in Moss stitch, blocked.

Savitri

Notes:

This striking jacket is worked from the bottom up in pieces, and then seamed together before adding the collar. The seams add stability and prevent the bulky weight yarn from stretching out of shape.

It is essential to read all instructions before beginning, especially when working the Right front: in this section, the buttonhole placement is worked at the same time as other shaping, and special attention is needed in those areas.

This garment has a dramatic armhole bind off, and creates a more fitted version of a modified drop shoulder garment. The tops of the sleeves are worked evenly for a specific length in order to fit into the cast-off areas of the armhole shaping. Any adjustments to the sleeve length must still have 1 (1.25, 1.25, 1.75, 1.75, 2.25, 2.25, 3.25)" of even work at the top.

This garment uses buttonholes with an extra yarn over, to create a buttonhole large enough for the oversized buttons. On the WS row after working a buttonhole row, drop the extra yarn over and work the buttonhole as one stitch.

Notes on Sizing: Throughout this pattern, there are notes to mathematically rework increases or decreases if you are altering the pattern sizing. Please note that any changes to the number of increases or decreases will alter the finished garment, so it will no longer match the schematic or measurements included with this pattern. It is highly recommended to sit down with the pattern and work out all adjustments according to the body measurements desired before beginning to work the pattern.

Dec 1: Decrease 1 stitch by either k2tog, ssk or p2tog. See pattern notes on recommended decrease.

Garter Selvedge Stitch:
Row 1: K1
Row 2: K1

Moss Stitch (worked flat)
Row 1: *K1, P1; rep from * to last stitch, K1
Row 2: *P1, K1; rep from * to last stitch, P1
Row 3: *P1, K1; rep from * to last stitch, P1
Row 4: *K1, P1; rep from * to last stitch, K1

Tips on working decreases in Moss stitch

First decrease in row: if 2nd stitch from the needle is a purl stitch, k2tog, otherwise p2tog.

Second decrease in row: if 2nd stitch from needle is a purl stitch, ssk, otherwise p2tog.

Right Ribbed Cable (worked flat over 15 sts)
Row 1: P2, *K1, P1; rep from * 4 times, K1, P2
Row 2: K2, *P1, K1; rep from * 4 times, P1, K2
Rows 3-10: Rep Rows 1-2
Row 11: P2, slip next 6 stitches onto cable needle and hold in back of work, work 5 stitches in pattern from circular needle, slip single purl stitch from left tip of cable needle onto left tip of circular

needle and p, work across remaining stitches from cable needle from right to left in pattern
Row 12: Rep Row 2

Left Ribbed Cable (worked flat over 15 sts)
Row 1: P2, *K1, P1; rep from * 4 times, K1, P2
Row 2: K2, *P1, K1; rep from * 4 times, P1, K2
Rows 3-10: Rep Rows 1-2
Row 11: P2, slip next 6 stitches onto cable needle and hold in front of work, work 5 stitches in pattern from circular needle, slip single purl stitch from left tip of cable needle onto left tip of circular needle and p, work across remaining stitches from cable needle from right to left in pattern
Row 12: Rep Row 2

Cable Increase (worked flat, increases 10 sts to 15 sts)
Row 1: P2, *K1fb; rep from * 4 times, K1, P2 (15 sts)
Row 2: K2, *P1, K1; rep from * 4 times, P1, K2

Cable Decrease (worked flat)
Row 1: P2, *K2tog; rep from * 4 times, K1, P2 (10 sts)
Row 2: K2, P6, K2

Buttonhole (worked flat)
Row 1: Work to 19 (21, 25, 27, 29, 31, 31, 33) sts before marker, yo, yo, dec 1. If 2nd stitch from needle is a purl stitch, k2tog, otherwise p2tog. On next row after buttonhole, drop extra yo and work the buttonhole as one stitch.

Cable Cast-on
*Insert needle into space between the first and second stitches on the needle, yarn over and pull a stitch through, twist to the right and place stitch on the needle through the back of the loop; rep from * for remainder of cast on.

DIRECTIONS
Back
Cast on 73 (79, 85, 93, 99, 107, 113, 121) sts.
Work 9 rows in Moss stitch.

Cable Setup Row (WS): K8 (10, 11, 14, 16, 19, 22, 25), pm, K10, pm, work Moss stitch as established over following 37 (39, 43, 45, 47, 49, 49, 51) sts, pm, K10, pm, K8 (10, 11, 14, 16, 19, 22, 25).

Cable Increase Row 1 (RS): K1, work St st to marker, sm, work Cable Increase Row 1, sm, work Moss stitch as established to next marker, sm, work Cable Increase Row 1, sm, work St st to last stitch, K1. 83 (89, 95, 103, 109, 117, 123, 131) sts

Cable Increase Row 2 (WS): K1, work St st to marker, sm, work Cable Increase Row 2, sm, work Moss stitch as established to next marker, sm, work Cable Increase Row 2, sm, work St st to last stitch, K1.

Next Row (RS): K1, work St st to marker, sm, work next row of Left Ribbed Cable, sm, work Moss stitch as established to next marker, sm, work next row of Right Ribbed Cable Ro, sm, work St st to last stitch, K1.

Continue working evenly in pattern as established, repeating Rows 1-12 of Left- and Right Ribbed Cable patterns between the stitch markers, until piece measures 2.5 (2.5, 3.5, 3.5, 4.5, 4.75, 5.5, 5.75)" from cast on edge.

Note on Sizing: If you are adjusting length, this is the area to add or remove length. Make sure to add or subtract the difference in length for all following length measurements.

If you are adjusting circumference: each decrease uses 0.75" of length and reduces the circumference by 1.15". If you are removing decreases to create a larger waist circumference, you need to work an additional 0.75" before beginning the decreases. Likewise, if you are adding decreases, you need to work 0.75" less before beginning decreases.

Dec Row: Work in pattern as established to 2nd marker, sm, dec 1, work in pattern to 2 sts before next marker, dec 1, sm, work to end in pattern. 81 (87, 93, 101, 107, 115, 121, 129) sts

Working in pattern as established, rep Dec Row every 4 rows 6 more times. 69 (75, 81, 89, 95, 103, 109, 117) sts

Work evenly in pattern as established until piece measures 13 (12.5, 13, 12.5, 13.25, 12.75, 13, 12.75)" from cast on edge.

Note on Sizing: If you are adding increases to enlarge the bust circumference, remove 2 even rows from the repeat for every increase you add. If you are removing increases to decrease the bust size, the first increase row should still be worked at the indicated measurement in the pattern.

Inc Row: Work in pattern as established to 1 stitch before 1st marker, M1R, work in pattern to last marker, K1, M1L, work in pattern to end. 71 (77, 83, 91, 97, 105, 111, 119) sts

Working in pattern as established, rep Inc Row every 8 (8, 8, 8, 6, 6, 6, 6) rows one more time. 73 (79, 85, 93, 99, 107, 113, 121) sts

Work evenly in pattern as established until piece measures 18 (18, 18.5, 18.5, 19, 19, 19.5, 19.5)" from cast on edge.

Armhole Shaping: Bind off 3 (4, 4, 6, 6, 8, 8, 11) sts at beg of each of next 2 rows. 67 (71, 77, 81, 87, 91, 97, 99) sts

Work evenly in pattern, with one stitch on either end as garter selvedge stitch, until piece measures 6.5 (7, 7.5, 8, 8.5, 9, 9.5, 10)" from Armhole bind off.

Neck Shaping: Work in pattern to 2nd marker, remove marker and join new ball of yarn. Bind off 23 (25, 29, 31, 33, 35, 35, 37) sts, remove next marker, work to end in pattern. 22 (23, 24, 25, 27, 28, 31, 31) sts on each shoulder

Next Row (WS): Work in pattern.
Next Row (RS): Work Cable Decrease Row across first 15 stitches, work to end. 17 (18, 19, 20, 22, 23, 26, 26) sts

Bind off all stitches on WS.

Rep last two rows and bind off for other shoulder.

Right Front
Cast on 55 (59, 64, 69, 73, 78, 81, 86) sts.
Work 9 rows in Moss stitch.

Cable Setup Row (WS): K8 (10, 11, 14, 16, 19, 22, 25), pm, K10, pm, work Moss stitch as established over following 37 (39, 43, 45, 47, 49, 49, 51) sts.

Cable Increase Row 1 (RS): Work Moss stitch as established to marker, sm, work Cable Increase Row 1, sm, work St st to last stitch, K1. 60 (64, 69, 74, 78, 83, 86, 91) sts

Cable Increase Row 2 (WS): K1, work St st to marker, sm, work Cable Increase Row 2, sm, work Moss stitch as established to end.

Next Row (RS): Work Moss stitch as established to marker, sm, work next row of Right Ribbed Cable, sm, work St st to last stitch, K1.

Continue working evenly in pattern as established, repeating Rows 1-12 of Right Ribbed Cable pattern between the stitch markers, until piece measures 2.5 (2.5, 3.5, 3.5, 4.5, 4.75, 5.5, 5.75)" from cast on edge.

Dec Row: Dec 1, work in pattern to 2 sts before next marker, dec 1, sm, work to end in pattern. 58 (62, 67, 72, 76, 81, 84, 89) sts

Working in pattern as established, rep Dec Row every 4 rows 6 more times. 46 (50, 55, 60, 64, 69, 72, 77) sts

AT THE SAME TIME: When piece measures 9.5 (8.5, 9, 8, 9, 8, 8, 7.5)" from cast on edge work 1st buttonhole.

When piece measures 11.5 (11, 11.5, 11, 11.75, 11.25, 11.5, 11.25)" from cast on edge work 2nd buttonhole.

Work evenly in pattern as established until piece measures 13 (12.5, 13, 12.5, 13.25, 12.75, 13, 12.75)" from cast on edge, ending with a WS row.

Front Shaping Row (RS): Bind off 19 (21, 24, 27, 29, 31, 31, 33) sts, work in pattern to last marker, K1, M1L, work to end. 28 (30, 32, 34, 36, 39, 42, 45) sts

Work 2 rows in pattern as established.

Next Row (WS): Work to end in pattern, cast on 19 (21, 24, 27, 29, 31, 31, 33) sts using Cable Cast on. 47 (51, 56, 61, 65, 70, 73, 78) sts

Work 4 (4, 4, 4, 2, 2, 2) rows evenly in pattern.

Inc Row (RS): Work in pattern to 2nd marker, K1, M1L, work in pattern to end. 48 (52, 57, 62, 66, 71, 74, 79) sts

Work evenly in pattern as established until piece measures 1" from Cable Cast on edge at Front Shaping, ending with a WS row.

Next Row (RS): Work 3rd buttonhole.

Work evenly in pattern as established until piece measures 3.5 (4, 4, 4.5, 4.25, 4.75, 5, 5.25)" from Cable cast on edge at Front Shaping, ending with a WS row.

Next Row (RS): Work 4th buttonhole.

Work evenly in pattern as established until piece measures 18 (18, 18.5, 18.5, 19, 19, 19.5, 19.5)" from Cable cast on edge at Front Shaping, ending with a RS row.

Armhole Shaping: Bind off 3 (4, 4, 6, 6, 8, 8, 11) sts at beg of next row. 45 (48, 53, 56, 60, 63, 66, 68) sts

Working 1 garter selvedge stitch at armhole edge work even in pattern until piece measures 5 (5.5, 6, 6.5, 7, 7.5, 8, 8.5)" from Armhole Bind off ending with a WS row.

Collar Shaping (RS): Bind off 9 (10, 12, 13, 14, 15, 15, 16) sts, work to end. 36 (38, 41, 43, 46, 48, 51, 52) sts.

Work 2 rows evenly in pattern.

Next Row (WS): Work to end in pattern, cast on 9 (10, 12, 13, 14, 15, 15, 16) sts using Cable cast on. 45 (48, 53, 56, 60, 63, 66, 68) sts.

Work evenly in pattern until piece measures 6.5 (7, 7.5, 8, 8.5, 9, 9.5, 10)" from Armhole Bind off, ending with a WS row.

Cable Decrease Row: Work in pattern to marker, sm, work Cable Decrease Row 1, sm, work in pattern to end. 40 (43, 48, 51, 55, 58, 61, 63) sts

Next Row (WS): Bind off 17 (18, 19, 20, 22, 23, 26, 26) sts, remove marker, work in pattern to end. Leave yarn attached and move remaining 23 (25, 29, 31, 33, 35, 35, 37) sts on holder or waste yarn.

Left Front
Cast on 55 (59, 64, 69, 73, 78, 81, 86) sts.
Work 9 rows in Moss stitch.

Cable Setup Row (WS): Work Moss stitch as established over following 37 (39, 43, 45, 47, 49, 49, 51) sts, pm, K10, pm, K8 (10, 11, 14, 16, 19, 22, 25).

Cable Increase Row 1 (RS): K1, work St st to marker, sm, work Cable Increase Row 1, sm, work Moss stitch as established to end. 60 (64, 69, 74, 78, 83, 86, 91) sts

Cable Increase Row 2 (WS): Work Moss stitch as established to next marker, sm, work Cable Increase Row 2, sm, work St st to last stitch, K1.

Next Row (RS): K1, work St st to marker, sm, work next row of Left Ribbed Cable, sm, work Moss stitch as established to end.

Continue working evenly in pattern as established, repeating Rows 1-12 of Left Ribbed Cable pattern between the stitch markers, until piece measures 2.5 (2.5, 3.5, 3.5, 4.5, 4.75, 5.5, 5.75)" from cast on edge.

Dec Row: Work in pattern as established to 2nd marker, sm, dec 1, work in pattern to 2 sts before end, dec 1. 58 (62, 67, 72, 76, 81, 84, 89) sts

Working in pattern as established, rep Dec Row every 4 rows 6 more times. 46 (50, 55, 60, 64, 69, 72, 77) sts

Work evenly in pattern as established until piece measures 13 (12.5, 13, 12.5, 13.25, 12.75, 13, 12.75)" from cast on edge.

Inc Row: Work in pattern as established to 1 stitch before 1st marker, M1R, work in pattern to end. 47 (51, 56, 61, 65, 70, 73, 78) sts

Working in pattern as established, rep Inc Row every 8 (8, 8, 8, 6, 6, 6, 6) rows one more time. 48 (52, 57, 62, 66, 71, 74, 79) sts

Work evenly in pattern as established until piece measures 17 (17, 17.5, 17.5, 18, 18, 18.5, 18.5)" from cast on edge, ending with a WS row.

Buttonhole Row (RS): Work in pattern to last 6 sts, dec 1, yo, work in pattern to end.

Work evenly in pattern as established until piece measures 18 (18, 18.5, 18.5, 19, 19, 19.5, 19.5)" from cast on edge ending with a WS row.

Armhole Shaping: Bind off 3 (4, 4, 6, 6, 8, 8, 11) sts at beg of next row. 45 (48, 53, 56, 60, 63, 66, 68) sts

Working 1 garter selvedge stitch at armhole edge, work evenly in pattern until piece measures 5 (5.5, 6, 6.5, 7, 7.5, 8, 8.5)" from Armhole Bind off, ending with a RS row.

Collar Shaping (WS): Bind off 9 (10, 12, 13, 14, 15, 15, 16) sts, work to end. 36 (38, 41, 43, 46, 48, 51, 52) sts.

Work 2 rows evenly in pattern.

Next Row (RS): Work to end in pattern, cast on 9 (10, 12, 13, 14, 15, 15, 16) sts using the Cable cast on method. 45 (48, 53, 56, 60, 63, 66, 68) sts

Work evenly in pattern until piece measures 6.5 (7, 7.5, 8, 8.5, 9, 9.5, 10)" from Armhole Bind off, ending with a WS row.

Cable Decrease Row (RS): Work in pattern to marker, sm, work Cable Decrease Row 1, sm, work in pattern to end. 40 (43, 48, 51, 55, 58, 61, 63) sts

Next Row (WS): Work to marker, remove marker, bind off 17 (18, 19, 20, 22, 23, 26, 26) sts. Place remaining 23 (25, 29, 31, 33, 35, 35, 37) sts on holder or waste yarn.

Sleeves
Left Cuff
Cast on 57 (57, 59, 59, 61, 61, 63, 63) sts.
Work 4 rows in Moss stitch.

Buttonhole Row (RS): Work 4 sts in pattern, yo, yo, dec 1, work in pattern to last 2 sts, dec 1. 56 (56, 58, 58, 60, 60, 62, 62) sts

Work 3 rows evenly in pattern.

Next Row (RS): Bind off 10 sts, work in pattern to last 2 sts, dec 1. 45 (45, 47, 47, 49, 49, 51, 51) sts

Work 2 rows evenly in pattern.

Next Row (WS): Work in pattern to end of row, cast on 10 sts using Cable Cast on method. 55 (55, 57, 57, 59, 59, 61, 61) sts
Next Row (RS): Work to last 2 sts, dec 1. 54 (54, 56, 56, 58, 58, 60, 60) sts

Work 3 rows evenly in pattern.

Buttonhole Row (RS): Work 4 sts in pattern, yo, yo, dec 1, work in pattern to last 2 sts, dec 1. 53 (53, 55, 55, 57, 57, 59, 59) sts

Work 3 rows evenly in pattern.

Next Row (RS): Bind off 10 sts, work in pattern to end. 43 (43, 45, 45, 47, 47, 49, 49) sts
Next Row (WS): Bind off 2 sts, K to end. 41 (41, 43, 43, 45, 45, 47, 47) sts
Next Row (RS): K across.

Sleeve Body (use for both sleeves)

The RS and the WS reverse between the end of the cuff and the beginning of the sleeve body. The last row of each Cuff is a RS row and the first row of the sleeve body is also a RS row.

Row 1 (RS): K across. 41 (41, 43, 43, 45, 45, 47, 47) sts
Row 2 (WS): K1, P to last stitch, K1.
Inc Row (RS): K2, M1L, work St st to last 2 sts, M1R, k2. 43 (43, 45, 45, 47, 47, 49, 49) sts.

Working 1 garter selvedge stitch and remaining stitches in St st as established, rep Inc Row every 20 (12, 10, 8, 8, 6, 6, 6) rows 3 (5, 6, 7, 8, 10, 10, 11) more times. 49 (53, 57, 59, 63, 67, 71, 73) sts

Work Inc Row once more. 51 (55, 59, 61, 65, 69, 73, 75) sts

Work even in St st with one garter selvedge stitch on either side of work until piece measures 17 (17, 17.5, 17.5, 18, 18, 18.5, 18.5)" from turning edge. Bind off all stitches, cut yarn leaving a tail one and a half times as wide as the sleeve top.

Note on Sizing: If you are shortening the length, the sleeve must still have 1 (1.25, 1.25, 1.75, 1.75, 2.25, 2.25, 3.25)" of even work at the top. Removing 2 rows from a decrease repeat will remove 0.40" of length. Begin by removing rows from the decreases furthest from the cuff and remove as many rows as needed to reach your desired shortened length. A formula for this is length needed to remove / 0.40 = number of decreases need to lose 2 rows within the evenly worked rows between increases.

Right Cuff

Cast on 57 (57, 59, 59, 61, 61, 63, 63) sts.
Work 4 rows in Moss stitch.

Buttonhole Row (RS): Dec 1, work in pattern to last 6 sts, dec 1, yo, work to end. 56 (56, 58, 58, 60, 60, 62, 62) sts

Work 3 rows evenly in pattern.

Next Row (RS): Dec 1, work in pattern to end. 55 (55, 57, 57, 59, 59, 61, 61) sts

Next Row (WS): Bind off 10 sts, work in pattern to end. 45 (45, 47, 47, 49, 49, 51, 51) sts

Work 2 rows evenly in pattern.

Next Row (RS): Dec 1, work in pattern to end of row, cast on 10 sts using Cable Cast on method. 54 (54, 56, 56, 58, 58, 60, 60) sts

Work 3 rows evenly in pattern.

Buttonhole Row (RS): Dec 1, work in pattern to last 6 sts, dec 1, yo, work to end. 53 (53, 55, 55, 57, 57, 59, 59) sts

Work 3 rows evenly in pattern.

Next Row (RS): Bind off 2 sts, work in pattern to end. 51 (51, 53, 53, 55, 55, 57, 57) sts
Next Row (WS): Bind off 10 sts, K to end. 41 (41, 43, 43, 45, 45, 47, 47) sts

Next Row (RS): K across.

Work Sleeve body same as for Left Sleeve.

Finishing

Using Tapestry needle and tails from back bind off, seam back shoulders to corresponding front shoulders.

Seam sleeves by using tail from sleeve bind off as follows: using tapestry needle run yarn 1 (1.25, 1.25, 1.75, 1.75, 2.25, 2.25, 3.25)" down from top of sleeve through garter selvedge stitch. Seam topmost 1 (1.25, 1.25, 1.75, 1.75, 2.25, 2.25, 3.25)" of sleeve to bound off stitches of armhole shaping, seam bound off top edge of sleeve to garter stitch selvedge edge of armhole opening, seam topmost 1 (1.25, 1.25, 1.75, 1.75, 2.25, 2.25, 3.25)" of other side of sleeve to remaining bound off stitches of armhole shaping. Repeat for other sleeve.

Using Tapestry needle, seam sides of back to corresponding side of fronts. Seam sleeves from beginning of sleeve body, this includes the garter stitch row seen on the RS of the work but does not include the bound off 2 or 10 sts that are part of the cuff.

Collar

Right Front

Place held 23 (25, 29, 31, 33, 35, 35, 37) stitches onto needle and begin working RS where yarn is still attached.

Work 3 rows in pattern.

Short Row 1 (RS): Work in pattern to last stitch, w&t.
Short Row 2 (WS): Work to end in pattern.
Short Row 3: Work to 1 st before last wrap, w&t.
Short Row 4: Work to end in pattern.
Rep last 2 rows once more. (3 wraps worked)

Next Row (RS): Work across in pattern, lifting and working wraps in using Moss stitch.

Work evenly in pattern as established until piece reaches to centre back of collar, ending with either a Row 2 or Row 4 of Moss stitch pattern. Cut yarn and place all stitches onto a holder.

Left Front

Place held 23 (25, 29, 31, 33, 35, 35, 37) stitches onto needle and attach yarn to begin working RS.

Work 2 rows in pattern.

Short Row 1 (WS): Work in pattern to last stitch, w&t.
Short Row 2 (RS): Work to end in pattern.
Short Row 3: Work to 1 st before last wrap, w&t.
Short Row 4: Work to end in pattern.
Rep last 2 rows once more. (3 wraps worked)

Next Row (WS): Work across in pattern, lifting and working wraps in using Moss stitch.

Work evenly in pattern as established until piece reaches to centre back of collar. If left collar ended with Row 2, end right collar with Row 4, and vice versa.

With WS facing, join the collar using a 3-needle bind off. The WS is technically the WS according to the left and right fronts, but since the collar reverses, this will be the RS of the collar facing each other when seamed.

Using Tapestry needle, seam the collar to the back neck, and work in any loose ends.

Block collar with steam to set seam and shape.

Buttons

Fold cuff of sleeve to outside of sleeve overlapping button bands with other side of cuff. Cuff is designed to increase at same rate as sleeve to fit without pinching of sleeve. Place buttons for sleeve to align with holes on bands the same distance from the edge of the cuff, this will angle the top of cuff wider to fit over sleeve increases.

Attach buttons to Left Front to align with buttonholes on Right Front, attach button on inside of Right front to align with buttonhole on Left Front. If desired attach optional sewn on snap to inside of Right front and outside of Left front directly beside wide cut in front band.

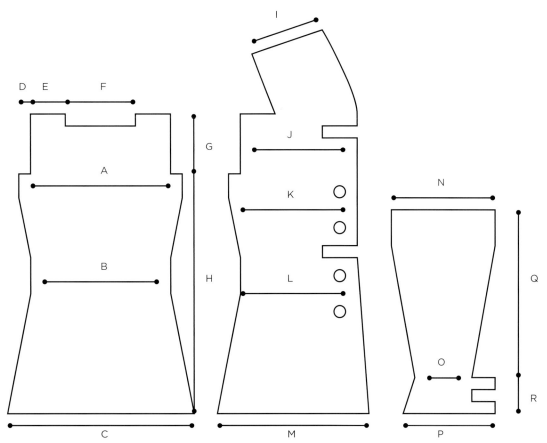

A 18 (19.75, 21.5, 23.75, 25.5, 27.75, 29.7, 31.75)"
B 16.75 (18.5, 20.25, 22.5, 24.25, 26.5, 28.25, 30.5)"
C 20.75 (22.5, 24.25, 26.5, 28.25, 30.5, 32.25, 34.5)"
D .75 (1, 1, 1.75, 1.75, 2.25, 2.25, 3)"
E 4.75 (5, 5.5, 5.75, 6.25, 6.5, 7.5, 7.5)"
F 6.5 (7, 8.25, 8.75, 9.5, 10, 10, 10.5)"
G 7 (7.5, 8, 8.5, 9, 9.5, 10, 10.5)"
H 18 (18, 18.5, 18.5, 19, 19, 19.5, 19.5)"
I 6.5 (7, 8.25, 8.75, 9.5, 10, 10, 10.5)"
J 8.75 (9.5, 10.25, 10.75, 11.75, 12.25, 13, 13.5)"
K 12.25 (13.5, 14.75, 16.25, 17.5, 18.75, 19.75, 21)"
L 11.75 (12.75, 14.25, 15.75, 16.75, 18.25, 19, 20.5)"
M 15.75 (16.75, 18.25, 19.75, 20.75, 22.25, 23, 24.5)"
N 14.5, 15.75, 16.75, 17.5, 18.5, 19.75, 20.75, 21.5)"
O 11.75 (11.75, 12.25, 12.25, 12.75, 12.75, 13.5, 13.5)"
P 16.25 (16.25, 16.75, 16.75, 17.5, 17.5, 18, 18)"
Q 17 (17, 17.5, 17.5, 18, 18, 18.5, 18.5)"
R 7.25"

CABLE EMBRACE

by Rene Dickey

FINISHED MEASUREMENTS

32 (34, 36, 40, 44, 48, 52)" finished bust measurement; garment is meant to be worn with no ease.

YARN

Knit Picks City Tweed DK (55% Merino Wool, 25% Superfine Alpaca, 20% Donegal Tweed; 123 yards/50g): Porpoise 24538 10 (10, 11, 12, 14, 15, 17) skeins.

NEEDLES

US 5 (3.75 mm) straight or circular needles, or size to obtain gauge
US 6 (4 mm) straight or circular needles, or size to obtain gauge

US 5 (3.75 mm) 32" circular needle, or size to obtain gauge

NOTIONS

Yarn Needle
3 Stitch Markers
Cable needle
Seven 5/8" buttons with optional 1/2" button backs.

GAUGE

25 sts and 29 rows = 4"x4" in Cable Pattern, blocked (gauge swatch instructions below).
20 sts and 26 rows = 4"x4" in Reverse Stockinette Stitch, blocked.

Cable Embrace

Notes:

Special Abbreviations
BC: Back Cross; slip 2 sts onto cable needle, hold in back, k2, then k2 from cable needle.

FC: Front Cross; slip 2 sts onto cable needle, hold in front, k2, then k2 from cable needle.

sm: slip marker.

M1r: make one right; insert left-hand needle from back to front below running thread between the stitches and knit the stitch.

M1l: make one left; insert left-hand needle from front to back below running thread between the stitches and knit into the back of the stitch.

Rev St st: Reverse Stockinette Stitch; Purl on RS, Knit on WS.

2x2 Rib
RS: K1, *k2, p2; rep from * across, end k1.

WS: knit the knit sts and the purl stitches as they are presented

Cable Pattern for Gauge Swatch
Cast on 26 sts

Row 1 (and all WS rows): K3, p20, k3.

Row 2 (RS): P3, k6, BC, FC, k6, p3.

Row 4: P3, k4, BC, k4, FC, k4, p3.

Row 6: P3, k2, BC, k8, FC, k2, p3.

Row 8: P3, BC, k12, FC, p3

Notes: Each piece is knit separately and seamed at the end. The back is divided into 3 sections by stitch markers, with the cable panel in the middle and Reverse St st on each side. Each front is divided into 2 sections by a stitch marker, half the cable panel and Reverse St st on the side. The sleeves are knit in Reverse St st.

DIRECTIONS
Back
With smaller needles, CO 102 (110, 118, 126, 138, 154, 166) sts, placing stitch markers after 9 (13, 17, 21, 19, 19, 25) sts, 51 (55, 59, 63, 69, 77, 83) sts, and 93 (97, 101, 105, 119, 135, 141) sts.

Work 2x2 rib for 9 (9, 9, 9, 15, 15, 15) rows.

Change to larger needles.

Row 1 (RS): P to first marker, sm, K2, *k4, BC, rep from * to second marker, sm, *FC, k4, rep from* until two sts before third marker, k2, sm, p to end.

Row 2 (and all WS Rows): K to first marker, sm, p to third marker, sm, k to end.

Row 3: P to first marker, sm, *k4, BC, rep from * until two sts before second marker, k2, sm, k2, *FC, k4, rep from * to third marker, sm, p to end.

Row 5: P to first marker, sm, k2, *BC, k4, rep from * to second marker, sm, *k4, FC, rep from * until two sts before third marker, k2, sm, p to end.

Row 7: P to first marker, sm, *BC, k4, rep from * until two sts before second marker, k2, sm, k2, *k4, FC, rep from * to third marker, sm, p to end.

Repeat rows 1-8 for cable pattern until work measures 2 (2, 2, 2, 2.5, 2.5, 2.5)" from cast on edge ending with a RS row.

Waist Shaping:
Dec Row (WS): K2, ssk, work in pattern to last 4 sts, k2tog, k2.

Continuing in cable pattern, rep Dec Row every 12 (12, 12, 12, 10, 10, 10)th row 3 (3, 3, 3, 4, 4) more times. 94 (102, 110, 118, 128, 144, 156) sts.

Work evenly in cable pattern until work measures 8.5 (9, 9, 9, 9.5, 9.5, 9.5)" from cast on edge, ending with a RS row.

Inc Row (WS): K2, M1r, work in pattern to last 2 sts, M1l, k2.

Continuing in cable pattern, rep Inc Row every 10 (10, 10, 10, 8, 8, 8)th row 3 (3, 3, 3, 4, 4, 4) more times. 102 (110, 118, 126, 138, 154, 166) sts.

Work evenly in cable pattern until work measures 16.5 (17, 17, 17, 17.5, 17.5, 17.5)" from cast on edge, ending with a WS row.

Armhole Shaping:
Next 2 Rows: BO 4 (6, 6, 7, 7, 7, 7) sts at beg of each of next two rows.

Next 2 Rows: BO 2 (2, 3, 3, 3, 4, 4) sts at beg of each of next two rows. 90 (94, 100, 106, 118, 132, 144) sts.

Sizes 32, 34, 36, 40 only:
Next row (RS): Work evenly in cable pattern.

(WS): K1, ssk, work in pattern to last 3 sts, k2tog, k1.

Continuing in cable pattern, rep last two rows 2 (2, 3, 4) more times. 86 (90, 94, 98) sts.

Sizes 44, 48, 52 only:
Next two rows: BO 2 (2, 3) sts at beg of each of next two rows. 114 (128, 138) sts.

Next row (RS): Work evenly in cable pattern.

Next Row (WS): K1, ssk, work in pattern to last 3 sts, k2tog, k1.Continuing in cable pattern, rep last two rows 3 (4, 5) more times. 106 (118, 126) sts.

All Sizes:
Work evenly in cable pattern until work measures 23.5 (24.5, 24.5, 25, 26, 27, 27.5)" from cast on edge, ending with a WS row.

Back Neck and Shoulder Shaping:
Next Row (RS): BO 6 (7, 7, 7, 8, 10, 10) sts, work in pattern for 14 (14, 14, 15, 18, 20, 22)sts [15 (15, 15, 16, 19, 21, 23) sts on right-hand needle], BO next 46 (46, 50, 52, 52, 56, 60) sts [neck opening made], work in pattern to end of row.

Next Row (WS): BO 6 (7, 7, 7, 8, 10, 10) sts, work in pattern to neck opening, turn work.

Next Row (RS): K2, ssk, work in pattern to end.

Next Row (WS): BO 7 (7, 7, 7, 9, 10, 11) sts, work in pattern to end.

Next Row (RS): Work in pattern to end.

Next Row (WS): BO rem 7 (7, 7, 8, 9, 10, 11) sts.

With WS facing, attach yarn at left side of neck.

Next Row (WS): Work in pattern to end.

Next Row (RS): BO 7 (7, 7, 7, 9, 10, 11) sts, work in pattern to last 4 sts, k2tog, k2.

Next Row (WS): Work in pattern to end.

Next Row (RS): BO rem 7 (7, 7, 8, 9, 10, 11) sts.

Right Front

With smaller needles, CO 52 (56, 60, 64, 72, 80, 84) sts placing a stitch marker after 43 (43, 43, 43, 51, 59, 59) sts.

Work in 2x2 rib for 9 (9, 9, 9, 15, 15, 15) rows. You will end each row with a K3.

Change to larger needles.

Row 1 (RS): K1, *FC, k4, rep from *until two sts before marker, k2, sm, p to end.
Row 2 (and all WS Rows): K to marker, sm, p to end.
Row 3: K3, *FC, k4, rep from * to marker, sm, p to end.
Row 5: K1, *k4, FC, rep from *until two sts before marker, k2, sm, p to end.
Row 7: K3, *k4, FC, rep from * to marker, sm, p to end.

Repeat rows 1-8 for cable pattern until work measures 2 (2, 2, 2, 2.5, 2.5, 2.5)" from cast on edge, ending with a RS row.

Waist Shaping:
Dec Row (WS): K2, ssk, work in pattern to end.

Continuing in cable pattern, rep Dec Row every 12 (12, 12, 12, 10, 10, 10)th row 3 (3, 3, 3, 4, 4, 4) more times. 48 (52, 56, 60, 67, 75, 79) sts.

Work evenly in cable pattern until work measures 8.5 (9, 9, 9, 9.5, 9.5, 9.5)" from cast on edge ending with a RS row.

Inc Row (WS): K2, M1r, work in pattern to end.

Continuing in cable pattern, rep Inc Row every 10 (10, 10, 10, 8, 8, 8)th row 3 (3, 3, 3, 4, 4, 4) more times. 52 (56, 60, 64, 72, 80, 84) sts.

Work evenly in cable pattern until work measures 15.5 (16, 16, 16, 16.5, 17, 17)" from cast on edge, ending with a WS row.

Neck Shaping:
Next Row (RS): K1, ssk, work in pattern to end.

Continuing in cable pattern, rep Dec Row on every RS row 23 (24, 26, 27, 29, 31, 31) more times.

At the same time when work measures 16.5 (17, 17, 17, 17.5, 17.5, 17.5)" from cast on edge, begin armhole shaping.

Next Row (WS): BO 4 (6, 6, 7, 7, 7, 7) sts, work in pattern to end.

Next Row (RS): Work in pattern to end.
Next Row (WS): BO 2 (2, 3, 3, 3, 4, 4) sts, work in pattern to end.
Next Row (RS): Work in pattern to end.

Sizes 32, 34, 36, 40 only:
Next Row (WS) : K1, ssk, work in pattern to end.
Next Row(RS): Work evenly in cable pattern.

Continuing in cable pattern, rep last two rows 1 (1, 2, 3) more times.

Sizes 44, 48, 52 only:
Next Row (WS): BO 2 (2, 3) sts, work in pattern to end.
Next Row (RS): Work in pattern to end.
Next Row (WS): K1, ssk, work in pattern to end.

Next Row (RS): Work evenly in cable pattern.

Continuing in cable pattern, rep last two rows 3 (4, 5) more times.

When all neck and armhole shaping is complete 20 (21, 21, 22, 26, 30, 32) sts remain.

All Sizes:
Work evenly in cable pattern until work measures 23.5 (24.5, 24.5, 25, 26, 27, 27.5)" from cast on edge, ending with a RS row.

Next Row (WS): BO 6 (7, 7, 7, 8, 10, 10) sts, work in pattern to end.
Next Row (RS): Work in pattern to end.
Next Row (WS): BO 7 (7, 7, 7, 9, 10, 11) sts, work in pattern to end.
Next Row (RS): Work in pattern to end.
Next Row (WS): BO rem 7 (7, 7, 8, 9, 10, 11) sts.

Left Front

With smaller needles, CO 52 (56, 60, 64, 72, 80, 84) sts, placing a stitch marker after 9 (13, 17, 21, 19, 19, 25) sts.

Work 2x2 rib for 9 (9, 9, 9, 15, 15, 15) rows. You will end each row with a K3.

Change to larger needles.

Row 1 (RS): P to marker, sm, K2, *k4, BC, rep from *, end k1.

Row 2 (and all WS Rows): P to marker, sm, k to end.
Row 3: P to marker, sm, *k4, BC, rep from *, end k3.
Row 5: P to marker, sm, k2,*BC, k4, rep from *, end k1.
Row 7: P to marker, sm, *BC, k4, rep from *, end k3.

Repeat rows 1-8 for cable pattern until work measures 2 (2, 2, 2, 2.5, 2.5, 2.5)" from cast on edge ending with a RS row.

Waist Shaping:

Dec Row (WS): Work in pattern to last 4 sts, k2tog, k2.

Continuing in cable pattern, rep Dec Row every 12 (12, 12, 12, 10, 10, 10)th row 3 (3, 3, 3, 4, 4, 4) more times. 48 (52, 56, 60, 67, 75, 79) sts.

Work evenly in cable pattern until work measures 8.5 (9, 9, 9, 9.5, 9.5, 9.5)" from cast on edge, ending with a RS row.

Inc Row (WS): Work in pattern to last 2 sts, M1l, k2.

Continuing in cable pattern, rep Inc Row every 10 (10, 10, 10, 8, 8, 8)th row 3 (3, 3, 3, 4, 4, 4) more times. 52 (56, 60, 64, 72, 80, 84) sts.

Work evenly in cable pattern until work measures 15.5 (16, 16, 16, 16.5, 17, 17)" from cast on edge, ending with a WS row.

Neck Shaping:

Next Row (RS): Work in pattern to last 3 sts, k2tog, k1.

Continuing in cable pattern, rep Dec Row on every RS row 23 (24, 26, 27, 29, 31, 31) more times.

At the same time when work measures 16.5 (17, 17, 17, 17.5, 17.5, 17.5)" from cast on edge, begin armhole shaping:

Next Row (RS): BO 4 (6, 6, 7, 7, 7, 7) sts, work in pattern to end.
Next Row (WS): Work in pattern to end.
Next Row (RS): BO 2 (2, 3, 3, 3, 4, 4) sts, work in pattern to end.

Sizes 32, 34, 36, 40 only:
Next Row (WS) : Work in pattern to last 3 sts, k2tog, k1.
Next Row (RS): work evenly in cable pattern.

Continuing in cable pattern, rep last two rows 1 (1, 2, 3) more times.

Sizes 44, 48, 52 only:
Next Row (RS): BO 2 (2, 3) st, work in pattern to end.
Next Row (WS): Work in pattern to end.
Next Row (RS): Work evenly in cable pattern.
Next Row WS): Work in pattern to last 3 sts, k2tog, k1.

Continuing in cable pattern, rep last two rows 3 (4, 5) more times.

When all neck and armhole shaping is complete 20 (21, 21, 22, 26, 30, 32) sts remain.

All Sizes:
Work evenly in cable pattern until work measures 23.5 (24.5, 24.5, 25, 26, 27, 27.5)" from cast on edge, ending with a WS row.

Shoulder Shaping:
Next Row (RS): BO 6 (7, 7, 7, 8, 10, 10) sts, work in pattern to end.
Next Row (WS): Work in pattern to end.
Next Row (RS): BO 7 (7, 7, 7, 9, 10, 11) sts, work in pattern to end.

Next Row (WS): Work in pattern to end.
Next Row (RS): BO rem 7 (7, 7, 8, 9, 10, 11) sts.

Sleeves (make two)

With smaller needles, CO 42 (42, 42, 42, 46, 46, 50) sts.

Work 2x2 rib row for 9 (9, 9, 9, 15, 15, 15) rows.

Change to larger needles, and begin working in Rev St st.

Next Row (RS): P to end.
Inc Row (WS): K2, M1r, k to last 2 sts, M1l, k2.

Continuing in Rev St st, rep Inc Row every 8 (8, 6, 6, 6, 4, 4)th row 10 (11, 14, 16, 16, 19, 20) more times. 64 (66, 72, 76, 80, 86, 92) sts.

Continue working in Rev St st until work measures 17.5 (18, 18, 18, 18, 18, 18.5)" from cast on edge ending with a WS row.

Cap Shaping:
Next 2 Rows: BO 4 (6, 6, 7, 7, 7, 7) sts at beg of each of next two rows.
Next 2 Rows: BO 2 (2, 3, 3, 3, 4, 4) sts at beg of each of next two rows. 52 (50, 54, 56, 60, 64, 70) sts.
Next Row (RS): Work in pattern.
Dec Row (WS): K2, ssk, k to last 4 sts, k2tog, k2.

Continuing in Rev St st pattern, rep Dec Row on every WS row 12 (12, 13, 14, 15, 17, 19) times more. 26 (24, 26, 26, 24, 24, 24) sts.

Next 2 Rows: BO 3 (2, 3, 3, 2, 2, 2) sts at beg of each of next two rows.

BO rem 20sts.

Finishing

Wash and block pieces to diagram.

Sew together shoulders.

Place a marker at the first neck dec on each front. Mark placement of 7 buttonholes on right front of garment. The first just above ribbing, the last at the first neck dec, and the other 5 spaced evenly between.

With RS facing, using smaller circular needles beg at CO edge of right front and pick up 80 (82, 82, 82, 84, 86, 86) sts to first marker, 45 (47, 47, 49, 51, 53, 55) sts to shoulder seam, 38 (42, 42, 42, 42, 46, 46) sts across back neck to left shoulder seam, 45 (47, 47, 49, 51, 53, 55) sts to second marker, and 80 (82, 82, 82, 84, 86, 86) sts to CO edge of left front; 288 (300, 300, 304, 312, 324, 328) sts.

Row 1(WS): P1 *p2, k2, rep from * end p3.
Row 2 (RS): K1 *k2, p2, rep from * end k3.

Sizes 44, 48, 52 only:
Rep rows 1 and 2.

All Sizes:
Next Row: (Button hole row) Work rib sts as row 1 making either a 3 st horizontal button hole or a yo, k2tog buttonhole at each marked buttonhole position.

Next Row (RS): Rep Row 2.
Next Row (WS): Rep Row 1.

Sizes 44, 48, 52 only:
Rep rows 2 and 1.

BO all sts in rib.

Sew in sleeve caps. Sew sleeve and side seams. Weave in all loose ends. Sew on buttons with optional button backs. Block again if desired and enjoy!

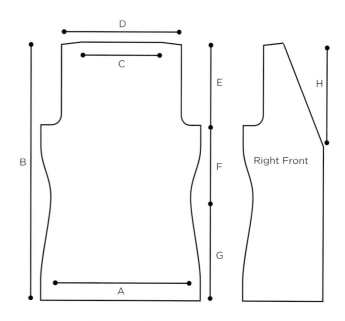

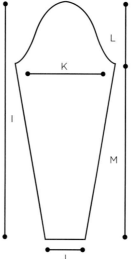

A 16 (17, 18, 20, 22, 24, 26)"
B 24 (25, 25, 25.5, 26.5, 27.5, 28)"
C 7.5 (8, 8, 8.5, 8.5, 9, 9.5)"
D 13.5 (14, 14.5, 15, 17, 18.5, 20)"
E 7.5 (8, 8, 8.5, 9, 10, 10.5)"
F 8"
G 8.5 (9, 9, 9.5, 9.5, 9.5)"
H 8.5 (9, 9, 9.5, 10, 10.5, 11)"
I 22.5 (23, 23, 23.5, 24, 24.5, 25.5)"
J 8 (8, 8, 8, 9, 9.5, 10)"
K 12.5 (13, 14, 14.5, 15.5, 17, 18.5)"
L 5 (5, 5, 5.5, 6, 6.5, 7)"
M 17.5 (18, 18, 18, 18, 18, 18.5)"

Abbreviations							
BO	bind off		and back of stitch	PU	pick up	SSP	sl, sl, p these 2 sts
cn	cable needle	K-wise	knitwise	P-wise	purlwise		tog tbl
CC	contrast color	LH	left hand	rep	repeat	SSSK	sl, sl, sl, k these 3 sts
CDD	Centered double	M	marker	Rev St st	reverse stockinette		tog
	dec	M1	make one stitch		stitch	St st	stockinette stitch
CO	cast on	M1L	make one left-lean-	RH	right hand	sts	stitch(es)
cont	continue		ing stitch	rnd(s)	round(s)	TBL	through back loop
dec	decrease(es)	M1R	make one right-	RS	right side	TFL	through front loop
DPN(s)	double pointed		leaning stitch	Sk	skip	tog	together
	needle(s)	MC	main color	Sk2p	sl 1, k2tog, pass	W&T	wrap & turn (see
EOR	every other row	P	purl		slipped stitch over		specific instructions
inc	increase	P2tog	purl 2 sts together		k2tog: 2 sts dec		in pattern)
K	knit	PM	place marker	SKP	sl, k, psso: 1 st dec	WE	work even
K2tog	knit two sts to-	PFB	purl into the front	SL	slip	WS	wrong side
	gether		and back of stitch	SM	slip marker	WYIB	with yarn in back
KFB	knit into the front	PSSO	pass slipped stitch	SSK	sl, sl, k these 2 sts	WYIF	with yarn in front
			over		tog	YO	yarn over

GRADUAL SCARF

by Cindy Garland

FINISHED MEASUREMENTS
12" (30cm) wide x 72" (183cm) long

YARN
Knit Picks Wool of the Andes Bulky
(100% Peruvian Highland Wool; 137
yards/100g):
MC Stormy 25555, 2 skeins; CC Cadet
25109, 2 Skeins.

NEEDLES
US 11 (8mm) straight or circular needles,
or size to obtain gauge

NOTIONS
Yarn Needle
2 Stitch Markers

GAUGE
10.75 sts and 17.5 rows = 4" in St st,
blocked.

Gradual Scarf

Notes:

Scarf is worked in stockinette and finished with garter stitch borders and ends. Pattern is written and striping sequence is visually charted.

Stitch Pattern (worked flat)

Row 1: Sl 1, K3, SM, K to last 4 sts, SM, K4.
Row 2: Sl 1, K3, SM, P to last 4 sts, SM, K4.

DIRECTIONS

With CC, loosely CO 32 sts.

Row 1-5: Sl 1, K to end
Row 6: Sl 1, K3, PM, K to last 4 sts, PM, K4.
Row 7: Sl 1, K3, SM, P to last 4 sts, SM, K4.

Repeat Rows 6 - 7 until completion of Row 304, at the same time, following Color Stripe Chart.

Row 305-309: Sl 1, K to end.

Bind Off Loosely.

Finishing

Weave in ends, wash and block to size.

Color Stripe Chart

CC	CO - R 23
MC	R 24 - 25
CC	R 26 - 47
MC	R 48 - 51
CC	R 52 - 71
MC	R 72 - 77
CC	R 78 - 95
MC	R 96 - 103
CC	R 104 - 119
MC	R 120 - 129
CC	R 130 - 143
MC	R 144 - 155
CC	R 156 - 167
MC	R 168 - 181
CC	R 182 - 191
MC	R 192 - 207
CC	R 208 - 215
MC	R 216 - 233
CC	R 234 - 239
MC	R 240 - 259
CC	R 260 - 263
MC	R 264 - 285
CC	R 286 - 287
MC	R 288 - 309/BO

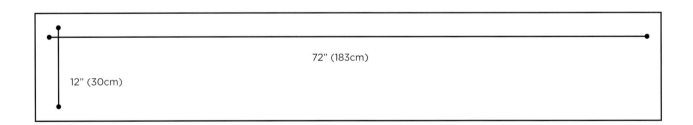

72" (183cm)

12" (30cm)

CALISTOGA

by Jill Wright

FINISHED MEASUREMENTS

32 (36, 40, 44, 48, 52, 56, 60, 64)"
finished bust measurement; garment is
meant to be worn with 2-4" of ease.
28.25 (28.75, 29.25, 29.75, 30.25, 30.75,
31.25, 31.75, 32.25)" total length

YARN

Knit Picks Capra DK (85% Merino Wool,
15% Cashmere; 123 yards/50g):
Caviar 24963, 11 (12, 13, 15, 16, 17, 18, 19, 21)
balls

NEEDLES

US 6 (4.00mm) circular needles or
straights as preferred, or size to obtain
gauge

NOTIONS

Yarn needle
Stitch holder or spare circular needle
Stitch marker
1 closed end zipper, 8" in length
Sewing needle
Matching thread

GAUGE

20 sts and 30 rows = 4" in Stockinette st,
blocked.

Calistoga

Notes:

Sweater is worked from the bottom up in pieces and seamed. Asymmetric collar is worked separately and sewn around neck edge.

Stockinette Stitch (worked flat, any number of sts)
Row 1 (RS): Knit.
Row 2: Purl.
Rep rows 1 and 2 for Stockinette st.

Reverse Stockinette Stitch (worked flat, any number of sts)
Row 1 (RS): Purl.
Row 2: Knit.
Rep rows 1 and 2 for Reverse Stockinette st.

Narrow Welts Pattern (worked flat, any number of sts)
Rows 1 and 2: Work in Stockinette st.
Rows 3 and 4: Work in Reverse Stockinette st.
Rep rows 1-4 for Narrow Welts pat.

Wide Welts Pattern (worked flat, any number of sts)
Rows 1-12: Work in Stockinette st.
Rows 13-24: Work in Reverse Stockinette st.
Rep rows 1-24 for Wide Welts pat.

M1K (Make 1 stitch knitwise)
PU the bar between st just worked and next st and place on LH needle (correct stitch mount). Knit through the back loop.

M1P (Make 1 stitch pwise)
PU the bar between st just worked and next st and place on LH needle (correct stitch mount). Purl through the back loop.

Back

CO 82 (92, 102, 112, 122, 132, 142, 152, 162) sts, and work in Narrow Welts pat for 2", ending after a Row 4.

Work in Stockinette st for 5" more, ending after a WS row.

Shape waist
Dec Row (RS): K5, ssk, k to last 7 sts, k2tog, k5.

Working in Stockinette st, rep Dec Row every 10 rows 4 more times – 72 (82, 92, 102, 112, 122, 132, 142, 152) sts.

Work evenly in Stockinette st until piece measures 16" from cast-on edge, ending after a WS row.

Inc Row (RS): K5, M1k, k to last 5 sts, M1k, k5.

Working in Stockinette st, rep Inc Row every 8 rows 4 more times – 82 (92, 102, 112, 122, 132, 142, 152, 162) sts.

Work evenly in Stockinette st until piece measures 21" from cast-on edge, ending after a WS row.

Shape Armholes
BO 4 (5, 6, 7, 8, 9, 10, 11, 12) sts at beg of each of next 2 rows.

Dec Row (RS): K2, ssk, k to last 4 sts, k2tog, k2.

Working in Stockinette st, rep Dec Row every RS row 3 (5, 7, 9, 11, 13, 15, 17, 19) more times – 66 (70, 74, 78, 82, 86, 90, 94, 98) sts.

Work evenly until armhole measures 6.5 (7, 7.5, 8, 8.5, 9, 9.5, 10, 10.5)", ending after a WS row.

Shape Shoulder
BO 2 (3, 4, 4, 5, 5, 6, 7, 7) sts at beg of each of next 2 rows.
BO 3 (3, 4, 5, 5, 6, 6, 7, 8) sts at beg of each of next 2 rows.
BO 3 (4, 4, 5, 6, 6, 7, 7, 8) sts at beg of each of next 2 rows.
BO rem 50 (50, 50, 50, 50, 52, 52, 52, 52) sts.

Front
Work same as Back through the Shape Waist Increases, then work evenly until piece measures 19.5 (19.75, 20, 20, 20.25, 20.25, 20.5, 20.75, 20.75)", ending after a WS row.

Shape Left Neck Edge
Place a marker at center of row, dividing sts in half.

Dec Row 1 (RS): Work in pat (including any bust incs that rem) to 4 sts before center marker, k2tog, k2, place rem sts on a holder or spare circular needle, remove marker, turn.

Row 2: Purl.
Dec Row 3: Work in pat to last 4 sts, k2tog, k2.
Row 4: Purl.
Rep Rows 3 and 4 only 18 (17, 16, 14, 13, 13, 12, 11, 9) times.
AT THE SAME TIME, when piece measures 21", shape armhole same as back on the armhole edge only. – 13 (16, 19, 23, 26, 28, 31, 34, 38) sts rem after neck and armhole shaping is complete.
Next row (dec row, RS): K to last 4 sts, k2tog, k2.

Working in Stockinette st, rep this dec every 4 rows 4 (5, 6, 8, 9, 10, 11, 12, 14) more times – 8 (10, 12, 14, 16, 17, 19, 21, 23) sts.

Work evenly until piece measures same as back to shoulder, then shape shoulder same as back.

Shape Right Neck Edge
Place all sts from holder back onto needle, and join yarn with RS facing.

Dec Row 1 (RS): K2, ssk, k to end.

Working in Stockinette st, rep Dec Row 1 every RS row 19 (18, 17, 15, 14, 14, 13, 12, 10) more times. AT THE SAME TIME, when piece measures 21", shape armhole same as back. – 13 (16, 19, 23, 26, 28, 31, 34, 38) sts rem after neck and armhole shaping is complete.

Continuing in Stockinette st, rep Dec Row 1 every 4 rows 5 (6, 7, 9, 10, 11, 12, 13, 15) more times – 8 (10, 12, 14, 16, 17, 19, 21, 23) sts.

Work evenly in Stockinette st until piece measures same as back to shoulder, then shape shoulder same as back.

Sleeves
CO 50 (52, 52, 54, 56, 58, 58, 60, 62) sts, and work in Wide Welts pat for 12 rows.

Working in Wide Welts pat Inc 1 st at each edge on next RS row.

Continuing in Wide Welts pat, inc 1 st at each edge every 18 (12, 8, 6, 6, 4, 4, 4, 4) rows 6 (9, 13, 16, 19, 22, 26, 29, 32) more times – 64 (72, 80, 88, 96, 104, 112, 120, 128) sts.

Work evenly in Wide Welts pat until piece measures 18", ending after a WS row.

Shape Sleeve Cap

Continuing in Wide Welts pat, BO 4 (5, 6, 7, 8, 9, 10, 11, 12) sts at beg of each of next 2 rows – 56 (62, 68, 74, 80, 86, 92, 98, 104) sts.

Working in Stockinette st, dec 1 st at each edge every row 4 (4, 6, 8, 8, 10, 12, 12, 14) times – 48 (54, 56, 58, 64, 66, 68, 74, 76) sts,

Continuing in Stockinette st, Dec 1 st at each edge every RS row 13 (16, 17, 18, 21, 22, 23, 26, 27) times – 22 sts.

BO all sts.

Make second sleeve same as first.

Collar

CO 21 sts.

Row 1 (RS): K5, [p4, k4] twice.
Row 2: [P4, k4] twice, p5.
Rep rows 1 and 2 until collar measures 6.5 (6.5, 6.5, 7, 7, 7, 7.5, 7.5, 7.5)", ending after a WS row.

Inc Row 1 (RS): K3, M1k, k2, * p2, M1P, p2, k2, M1k, k2; rep from * once more – 26 sts
Work evenly in established rib for 6.5 (6.5, 6.5, 7, 7, 7, 7.5, 7.5, 7.5)" more, ending after a WS row.

Inc Row 2 (RS): K3, M1k, k3, * p3, M1P, p2, k3, M1k, k2; rep from * once more – 31 sts
Work evenly in established rib for 6.5 (6.5, 6.5, 7, 7, 7, 7.5, 7.5, 7.5)" more, ending after a WS row.

Inc Row 3 (RS): K4, M1k, k3, * p3, M1P, p3, k3, M1k, k3; rep from * once more – 36 sts

Work evenly in established rib for 6.5 (6.5, 6.5, 7, 7, 7, 7.5, 7.5, 7.5)" more, ending after a WS row.

Inc Row 4 (RS): K4, M1k, k4, * p4, M1P, p3, k4, M1k, k3; rep from * once more – 41 sts.
Work evenly in established rib until collar measures 33 (33.25, 33.75, 34.75, 35, 36.25, 36.75, 37.25, 38.25)", then bind off all sts loosely.

Finishing

Weave in loose ends. Block pieces to measurements.

Sew shoulder seams.

Sew cast-on edge of collar from center point of V up right neck edge for 4". Pin side edge of collar around neckline from left side around to right, and sew in place. Pin RS of zipper to RS of left collar at outer Stockinette St edge, with matching thread sew this side of zipper in place from center point of V up left neck edge for 8". Sew other side of zipper underneath bound-off edge of collar.

Sew sleeves in place.

Sew sleeve and side seams.

Weave in any remaining loose ends.

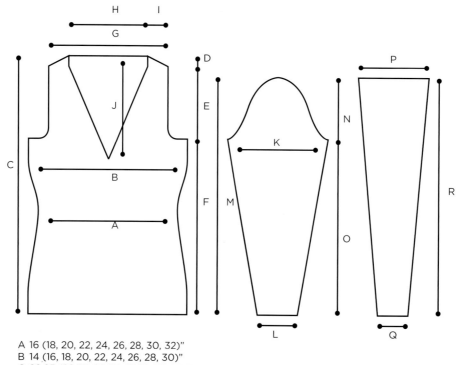

A 16 (18, 20, 22, 24, 26, 28, 30, 32)"
B 14 (16, 18, 20, 22, 24, 26, 28, 30)"
C 28.25 (28.75, 29.25, 29.75, 30.25, 30.75, 31.25, 31.75, 32.25)"
D .75"
E 6.5 (7, 7.5, 8, 8.5, 9, 9.5, 10, 10.5)"
F 21"
G 13 (13.5, 14.5, 15.5, 16, 16.75, 17.75, 18.25, 19.25)"
H 10.5 (10.5, 10.5, 10.5, 10.5, 10.75, 10.75, 10.75, 10.75)"
I 1.25 (1.5, 2, 2.5, 2.75, 3, 3.5, 3.75, 4.25)"
J 8.75 (9, 9.25, 9.75, 10, 10.5, 10.75, 11, 11.5)"
K 12.5 (14, 15.5, 17.25, 18.75, 20.5, 22, 23.5, 25.25)"
L 9.5 (10, 10, 10.5, 10.75, 11.25, 11.25, 11.5, 12)"
M 22.25 (23, 23.5, 24.25, 25, 25.5, 26, 26.75, 27.25)"
N 4.25 (5, 5.5, 6.25, 7, 7.5, 8, 8.75, 9.25)"
O 18"
P 8"
Q 4"
R 33 (33.25, 33.75, 34.75, 35, 36.25, 36.75, 37.25, 38.25)"

Abbreviations							
BO	bind off		and back of stitch	PU	pick up	SSP	sl, sl, p these 2 sts
cn	cable needle	K-wise	knitwise	P-wise	purlwise		tog tbl
CC	contrast color	LH	left hand	rep	repeat	SSSK	sl, sl, sl, k these 3 sts
CDD	Centered double	M	marker	Rev St st	reverse stockinette		tog
	dec	M1	make one stitch		stitch	St st	stockinette stitch
CO	cast on	M1L	make one left-lean-	RH	right hand	sts	stitch(es)
cont	continue		ing stitch	rnd(s)	round(s)	TBL	through back loop
dec	decrease(es)	M1R	make one right-	RS	right side	TFL	through front loop
DPN(s)	double pointed		leaning stitch	Sk	skip	tog	together
	needle(s)	MC	main color	Sk2p	sl 1, k2tog, pass	W&T	wrap & turn (see
EOR	every other row	P	purl		slipped stitch over		specific instructions
inc	increase	P2tog	purl 2 sts together		k2tog: 2 sts dec		in pattern)
K	knit	PM	place marker	SKP	sl, k, psso: 1 st dec	WE	work even
K2tog	knit two sts to-	PFB	purl into the front	SL	slip	WS	wrong side
	gether		and back of stitch	SM	slip marker	WYIB	with yarn in back
KFB	knit into the front	PSSO	pass slipped stitch	SSK	sl, sl, k these 2 sts	WYIF	with yarn in front
			over		tog	YO	yarn over

THICK CHILL

by Teresa Gregorio

Finished Measurements
33" circumference, 25" tall at longest point

Yarn
Knit Picks Wool of the Andes Bulky (100% Peruvian Highland Wool; 137 yards/100g): Silver 25107, 4 hanks.

Needles
US 15 (10mm) circular needles, or size to obtain gauge

Notions
Yarn Needle
Stitch Markers

Gauge
9 sts and 14 rows = 4" over stockinette in the round, blocked.

Thick Chill

Notes:

Thick Chill is an extreme knit; designed with large gauge, this cowl can stand up to the chilliest winds that Fall can whip! Holding two strands of Wool of the Andes Bulky at once, the use of large needles will create an accessory that is both a quick knit and an attractive, functional piece.

Simple in its appearance, Thick Chill utilizes short rows along the top of the hood to create a head-hugging curve, and decreases at the bottom of the cowl, keeping the edge slightly closer to the neck to prevent breezes sneaking up underneath.

Wrap and Turn

Keeping the yarn in the back, slip the stitch to be wrapped to the right needle. Bring the yarn forward between the needles, and slip the stitch back to the left needle.

There are written instructions accompanied by photographs demonstrating how to work a wrap and turn on both the knit side and purl side at the Purl Bee here: http://www.purlbee.com/short-row-tutorial/

You can also watch a video demonstrating the technique by Knitting Help here:
http://www.youtube.com/watch?v=G4GxFvi4KD0

DIRECTIONS
Working the Cowl

Holding two strands of yarn together at once, CO 75 sts. Being careful not to twist sts, join for knitting in the round.
Place a marker at the beginning of round.

K all 75 sts.

Cont to K all sts until piece measures 3" from CO.

Short Rows

RS: K until 10 sts before the end of the round, w&t 10th st.
WS: P all sts until 10 sts before the end of the round, w&t 10th st.
RS: K until 1 st before last wrapped st, w&t.
WS: P until 1 st before last wrapped st, w&t.

Rep last 2 rows 16 more times.
There are now 18 wrapped sts on each side of the cowl.

Picking Up Wraps

RS: K to wrapped st, *pick up wrap with st and K tog*, rep 17 more times, K to marker, sm, K 9 sts, *pick up wrap with st and K tog*, rep 17 more times, K to marker.

You are now working in the round.

K all 75 sts.
Cont to K all sts for 10".

Decreasing

K 23, K2tog, rep twice more.
There are now 72 sts.
K 3 rounds.

K 22, K2tog, rep twice more.
There are now 69 sts.
K 3 rounds.
Loosely cast off K-wise.

Finishing

Weave in ends, wash and block to diagram.

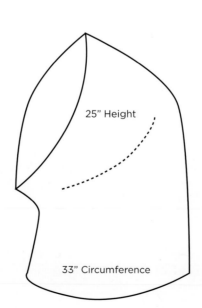

25" Height

33" Circumference

STRAIGHT A

by Sparrow Kelley

FINISHED MEASUREMENTS

30 (34, 38, 42, 46)" finished bust
measurement; garment is meant to
be worn with 1-2" of negative ease.
Measurements are for finished sized of
garment; to achieve negative ease, knit a
size down.

YARN

Knit Picks Capra DK (85% Merino Wool,
15% Cashmere; 123 yards/50g):
Platinum 24965, 7 (8, 9, 10, 11) balls.
Knit Picks Capretta (80% Merino
Wool, 10% Cashmere, 10% Nylon; 230
yards/50g): Platinum 25595, 1 ball

NEEDLES

US 8 (5mm) circular needles, or size to
obtain gauge
US 2 (3mm) circular needles

NOTIONS

Yarn Needle
2 Stitch markers
Scrap yarn or stitch holders

GAUGE

20 sts X 24 rows= 4" X 4", knit flat in
stockinette stitch and wet-blocked

Straight A

Notes:

Straight A is a simple A-line dress with seed stitch accents and a knit-in folded hem. Worked in luxurious Capra yarn, it's easy to knit and the perfect go-to sweater dress for any fall outfit!

Seed Stitch (worked flat, over an even number of sts)
Row 1: P1, K1
Row 2: P1, K1

Knit-In Folded Hem
The knit in folded hem technique is used at the cast on edge to help counteract the effects of curling stockinette. It is knit flat, and then seamed closed later.

With Capretta yarn and US8 needles, CO the number of sts needed for your size using a long tail cast on.
Row 1 (WS): K
Row 2 (RS): P
Repeat Rows 1-2 a total of 4 times.

Break Capretta yarn and attach Capra.
Row 9 (WS): K
Row 10 (RS): K
Row 11 (WS): P
Repeat Rows 10-11 a total of 4 times

Using the US2 circular needles, pick up stitches along the long tail cast on edge (see figure 1). Hold the US2 needle with picked up stitches behind the US8 needle, both in your left hand.

Figure 1

Row 18: Work the stitches together by knitting two together (one from each needle, being careful not to twist the picked up sts) across the whole row (see figure 2).

Figure 2

Figure 3

Bind Off
For this pattern you will be instructed to Bind Off and then pick up stitches later along the Bind Off edge. The bind off method used for this pattern is the traditional "pull one over" bind off. To pick up stitches, pull new yarn through the back loop created by this bind off method (see figure 4).

Figure 4

Move marker Right/Left

To work the Seed Stitch Chevron you will be instructed to Move marker Right or Left. To do this, slip the marker off the needle, work the next stitch (either to the right or left as instructed), and replace the marker in the new position.

DIRECTIONS

Cast on 190 (210, 234, 254, 278), work Knit-In Folded Hem. Place marker and join in the round, being careful not to twist.

Body (worked in the round)

Round 1: K95 (105, 117, 127,139), PM, K95 (105, 117, 127,139)

Round 2-11: K

Round 12: K1, K2tog, K to 2 sts before marker, SSK, SM, K1, K2tog, K to 2 sts before marker, SSK

Repeat Round 2-12 a total of 10 (10, 11, 11, 12) times (150 (170, 190, 210, 230) sts)

Round 1: K

Round 2: K1, M1, K to 1 st before marker, M1, K

Round 3-13: K

Round 14: K 77 (87, 97, 107, 117) sts, BO 75 (85, 95, 105, 115) sts across back

Front (worked flat)

Row 1 (RS): K1, SSK, K to 3 sts from end, K2TOG, K1 (75 (85, 95, 105, 115) sts)

Row 2 (WS): P

Row 3 (RS): K37 (42, 47, 52, 57), PM, K1, PM, K37 (42, 47, 52, 57)

Row 4 (WS): P

Seed Stitch Chevron Pattern

Row 1 (RS): K to marker, P1, K to end

Row 2 (WS): P to 1 st before marker, Move marker Left, [K1, P1] to marker, K1, Move marker Right, P to end

Row 3 (RS): K to 1 st before marker, Move marker Right, [P1, K1] to marker, P1, Move marker Left, K to end

Repeat rows 2-3 until markers reach last stitch.

Row 4-6: [P1, K1] to last st, ending with P1

Row 7(RS): [P1, K1] for 30 sts, BO 15 (25, 35, 45, 55) sts, [K1, P1] for 30 sts

Slip the first 30 sts onto a stitch holder or waste yarn. Continue with 30 sts on needles

Right Shoulder (Front)

Row 1 (WS): Work in established seed stitch to 2 sts from end, K2TOG

Row 2 (RS): Work in established seed stitch to end

Repeat rows 1-2 a total of 5 times (25 sts).

BO all sts and break yarn, leaving a long tail for seaming.

Left Shoulder (Front)

Replace 30 sts for left shoulder on needles.

Row 1 (WS): SSK, continue in established seed stitch to end

Row 2 (RS): Work in established seed stitch to end

Repeat rows 1-2 a total of 5 times (25 sts).

BO all sts and break yarn, leaving a long tail for seaming.

Back (worked flat)

With RS facing, pick up 74 (84, 94, 104, 114) sts along the back (through the back loop of BO edge stitches).

Row 1 (WS): [K1,P1] to end

Work in established seed stitch for 39 (45, 49, 55, 59) rows, ending with a WS row.

Next Row (RS): [P1, K1] for 30 sts, BO 14 (24, 34, 44, 54) sts, [K1, P1] for 30 sts

Slip the first 30 sts onto a stitch holder or waste yarn. Continue with 30 sts on needles

Left Shoulder (Back)

Row 1 (RS): Work in established seed stitch to 2 sts from end, K2TOG

Row 2 (WS): Work in established seed stitch to end

Repeat rows 1-2 a total of 5 times (25 sts).

BO all sts, DO NOT break yarn.
Turn and pick up 25 sts from edge just bound off.
Work in stockinette st for 10 rows.
BO all sts and break yarn, leaving a long tail for seaming.

Right Shoulder (Back)

Replace 30 sts for right shoulder on needles.

Row 1 (RS): SSK, continue in established seed stitch to end

Row 2 (WS): Work in established seed stitch to end

Repeat rows 1-2 a total of 5 times (25 sts).

BO all sts, DO NOT break yarn.
Turn and pick up 25 sts from edge just bound off.
Work in stockinette st for 10 rows.
BO all sts and break yarn, leaving a long tail for seaming.

Finishing

Turn the garment inside out. Seam the shoulders using yarn tails left during bind off.

Sew a seam from the start of the underarm (where sts split for bust) up 1". (This is to prevent gaping at the underarm.) Sew the gap at the cast on edge closed.

After seaming, pick up 60 (80, 100, 120, 140) sts along the neckline edge. Knit 1 round, then bind off.

Block (wet blocking is recommended), and work in ends.
Blocking dimensions from underarm to hem should be as follows:
30-34" size: 25"
38-42" size: 27"
46" size: 29"

After blocking, the hem might be a little rounded. If this is the case, gently press it on the wrong side with a steam iron. (DO NOT rub the iron over the fabric. This will cause it to felt.)

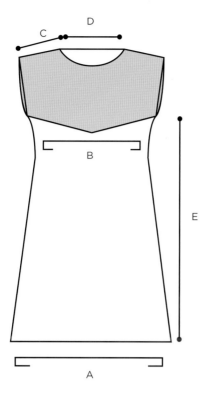

A 38 (42, 46.8, 50.8, 55.6)"
B 30 (34, 38, 42, 46)"
C 5"
D 5 (7, 9, 11, 13)"
E 20.2 (20.2, 22, 22, 23.8)"

Abbreviations	
BO	Bind Off
CO	Cast Off
K2tog	Knit 2 Together
M1	Make 1
PM	Place Marker
RS	Right Side
SSK	Slip, Slip, Knit
WS	Wrong Side
[]	Repeat this section

ATMOS CARDIGAN

by Hilary Smith Callis

FINISHED MEASUREMENTS

32.25 (36, 39.75, 44, 47.75, 52.5, 55.75, 60, 64.25)" finished bust measurement; garment is meant to be worn with 0-2" of negative ease.

YARN

Knit Picks Wool of the Andes Bulky (100% Wool; 137 yards/100g): Wallaby 25775, 6 (7, 8, 9, 9, 10, 11, 12, 12) skeins.

NEEDLES

US 9 (5.5mm) 30-60" circular needles (length needed depends on size)
US 9 (5.5mm) DPNs or two 24" circular needles for two circulars technique, or one 32" or longer circular needle for Magic Loop technique, or size to obtain gauge

US 10 (6mm) 30-60" circular needles, or size to obtain gauge

NOTIONS

Yarn Needle
2 Stitch Markers
Cable needle
Scrap yarn or stitch holder
8 (8, 8, 9, 9, 9, 9, 10, 10) buttons, size 1" in diameter

GAUGE

17 sts and 21 rows = 4" in cable patterns on US 10 (6mm) needles, blocked.
14 sts and 20 rows = 4" in Stockinette Stitch on US 10 (6mm) needles, blocked.
14 sts and 20 rows = 4" in 2x2 Ribbing on US 9 (5.5mm) needles, blocked.

For pattern support, contact xilary@gmail.com

Atmos Cardigan

Notes:

Atmos is worked from the bottom up in one piece to the armholes, after which the fronts and back are split and worked separately. The button bands are worked simultaneously with the rest of the cardigan over the first and last 8 stitches and the pockets are placed in the center of the Diamond Cables running up the fronts. The slightly puffed cap sleeves are picked up from the armholes and are shaped with short rows. The collar is picked up from the neck edge and is worked straight up in 2x2 Ribbing.

2x2 Ribbing (worked flat over a multiple of 4 sts):
Row 1: *K2, p2; rep from * to end.
Row 2: *P2, k2; rep from * to end.

C6B
Sl 3 sts to cable needle and hold in back of work; k3, k3 from cable needle.

C4F (C6F)
Sl 2 (3) sts to cable needle and hold in front of work; k2 (3), k2 (3) from cable needle.

C3BP
Sl 1 st to cable needle and hold in back of work; k2, p1 from cable needle.

C3FP
Sl 2 sts to cable needle and hold in front of work; p1, k2 from cable needle.

Plait Cable (worked flat over a multiple of 4 sts):
Row 1: C6F, k3.
Row 2 (and all even rows): P.
Rows 3: K.
Row 5: K3, C6B.
Row 7: K.

Diamond Cable Pattern (worked flat over 18 sts):
Row 1: P7, C4F, p7.
Rows 2, 4, and 6: K7, p4, k7.
Row 3: P7, k4, p7.
Row 5: Rep Row 1.
Row 7: P6, C3BP, C3FP, p6.
Row 8: K6, p2, k2, p2, k6.
Row 9: P5, C3BP, p2, C3FP, p5.
Row 10: K5, p2, k4, p2, k5.
Row 11: P4, C3BP, p4, C3FP, p4.
Row 12: K4, p2, k6, p2, k4.
Row 13: P3, C3BP, p6, C3FP, p3.
Row 14: K3, p2, k8, p2, k3.
Row 15: P2, C3BP, p8, C3FP, p2.
Row 16: K2, p2, k10, p2, k2.
Row 17: P1, C3BP, p10, C3FP, p1.
Row 18: K1, p2, k12, p2, k1.
Row 19: C3BP, k12, C3FP.
Row 20: P2, k14, p2.
Row 21: K2, p14, k2.
Row 22: Rep Row 20.

Row 23: C3FP, k12, C3BP.
Row 24: K1, p2, k12, p2, k1.
Row 25: P1, C3FP, p10, C3BP, p1.
Row 26: K2, p2, k10, p2, k2.
Row 27: P2, C3FP, p8, C3BP, p2.
Row 28: K3, p2, k8, p2, k3.
Row 29: P3, C3FP, p6, C3BP, p3.
Row 30: K4, p2, k6, p2, k4.
Row 31: P4, C3FP, p4, C3BP, p4.
Row 32: K5, p2, k4, p2, k5.
Row 33: P5, C3FP, p2, C3BP, p5.
Row 34: K6, p2, k2, p2, k6.
Row 35: P6, C3FP, C3BP, p6.
Row 36: K7, p4, k7.

Backwards Loop Cast On
Hold your needle in your right hand and grasp the working yarn in your left hand. Pass the working yarn around your left thumb from back to front. Slip the needle tip under the loop around your thumb. Pull your thumb out of the loop and tug on the working yarn to tighten up the stitch.

Short Rows (w&t)
Work until the stitch to be wrapped. If the next st is a knit st: bring yarn to the front of the work, slip next st as if to purl, return the yarn to the back; turn work and slip wrapped st onto right hand needle. Continue across row. If the next st is a purl st: bring yarn to the back of the work, slip next st as if to purl, return the yarn to the front; turn work and slip wrapped st onto right hand needle. Continue across row.

Picking up wraps: Work to the wrapped st. If the wrapped st is a knit st, insert the right hand needle under the wrap, then through the wrapped st kwise. Knit the wrap together with the wrapped st. If the wrapped st is a purl st, slip the wrapped st pwise onto the right hand needle, and use the left hand needle to lift the wrap and place it on the right hand needle. Slip wrap(s) and unworked st back to left hand needle; purl both together through the back loop.

DIRECTIONS
Body

Using 30-60" US 9 (5.5mm) circular needles, CO 146 (162, 178, 198, 214, 234, 246, 266, 282) sts. Do not join.

Next Row (WS): Set up button bands and ribbing: P2, k4, p2, *k2, p2; rep from * to last 6 sts, k4, p2. The first and last 8 sts will form the button bands and they will be worked in the pat as set above, incorporating buttonholes where necessary, until they are bound off at the neck edge.

Next Row (RS): K2, p4, k2, *p2, k2; rep from last * to last 6 sts, p4, k2.

Work in pat as set, knitting all k sts and purling all p sts, for 2 more rows.

Buttonhole Row 1 (WS): Work in pat as set to last 6 sts, k1, BO 2, p2.

Buttonhole Row 2: K2, p1, CO 2 sts using Backward Loop Method, p1, cont in pat as set to end.

Work in pat as set until piece measures 2.5" from CO edge slightly stretched, ending with a RS row.

The Buttonholes are created at the same time as you knit the rest of the cardigan. Please read the Buttonhole section below, then cont with the Body instructions.

Buttonholes

After the ribbing is complete, you will create 7 (7, 7, 8, 8, 8, 8, 9, 9) more buttonholes evenly along the right front button band as you knit the Body and complete the armholes.

To create buttonholes, rep Buttonhole Rows 1 and 2 as described above beg 3.75 (4, 4, 3.5, 3.5, 3.5, 3.75, 3.25, 3.25)" after the first Buttonhole, then every 3.75 (4, 4, 3.5, 3.5, 3.5, 3.5, 3.25, 3.25)" 6 (1, 1, 1, 3, 6, 6, 7, 7, 7) time(s), then every - (3.75, 3.75, 3.25, 3.25, 3.25, -, 3, 3)" - (5, 5, 4, 1, 1, -, 1, 1) time(s). The last buttonhole should fall roughly 0.5" before the neck BO row. If you lengthen or shorten the cardigan, be sure to adjust the length between the buttonholes as well.

Note: When measuring the length between buttonholes, measure from the BO edge in Buttonhole Row 1.

Next Row (WS): Work in pat, decreasing 1 (1, 1, 3, 3, 3, 1, 3, 1) st(s) with k2tog or p2tog anywhere in the piece. The exact placement of the decrease(s) does not matter. 145 (161, 177, 195, 211, 231, 245, 263, 281) sts.

Switch to US 10 (6mm) circular needles and set up cable patterns. Please note that sizes 47.75-64.25" have one more Plait Cable on each front and two more on the back than the other sizes.

Next Row (RS): K2, p4, k2, p1 (2, 2, 3, 3, 3, 3, 4, 4), k9, p8 (9, 9, 9, 9, 10, 10, 11), k4, p8 (10, 14, 18, 9, 9, 10, 10, 11), k0 (0, 0, 0, 9, 9, 9, 9, 9), p0 (0, 0, 0, 4, 9, 10, 14, 16), PM to mark left front, p1 (3, 7, 11, 4, 9, 10, 14, 16), k0 (0, 0, 0, 9, 9, 9, 9, 9), p0 (0, 0, 0, 2, 2, 3, 3, 4), k9, p8 (9, 9, 9, 9, 9, 10, 10, 11), k4, p8 (9, 9, 9, 9, 9, 10, 10, 11), k9, p8 (9, 9, 9, 9, 10, 10, 11), k4, p8 (9, 9, 9, 9, 9, 10, 10, 11), k9, p1 (3, 7, 11, 2, 3, 3, 4), k0 (0, 0, 0, 9, 9, 9, 9), p0 (0, 0, 0, 4, 9, 10, 14, 16),

PM to mark back, p1 (3, 7, 11, 4, 9, 10, 14, 16), k0 (0, 0, 0, 9, 9, 9, 9), p7 (7, 7, 7, 9, 9, 10, 10, 11), k4, p8 (9, 9, 9, 9, 9, 10, 10, 11), k9, p1 (2, 2, 2, 2, 2, 3, 3, 4), k2, p4, k2. 38 (42, 46, 51, 55, 60, 63, 68, 72) sts for each front and 69 (77, 85, 93, 101, 111, 119, 127, 137) sts for the back.

Next Row (WS): Work in pat as set, knitting all k sts and purling all p sts.

Beg cable patterns. If it will make it easier to keep track of the cable patterns, you may place markers around them.

Next Row (RS): K2, p4, k2, p1 (2, 2, 3, 3, 3, 3, 4, 4), work Row 1 of Plait Cable, p1 (2, 2, 2, 2, 2, 3, 3, 4), work Row 1 of Diamond Cable, p1 (3, 7, 11, 2, 2, 3, 3, 4), work Row 1 of Plait Cable 0 (0, 0, 0, 1, 1, 1, 1, 1) time(s), p0 (0, 0, 0, 4, 9, 10, 14, 16), SM, p1 (3, 7, 11, 4, 9, 10, 14, 16), work Row 1 of Plait Cable 0 (0, 0, 0, 1, 1, 1, 1, 1) time(s), p0 (0, 0, 0, 2, 2, 3, 3, 4), work Row 1 of Plait Cable, p1 (2, 2, 2, 2, 2, 3, 3, 4), work Row 1 of Diamond Cable, p1 (2, 2, 2, 2, 2, 3, 3, 4), work Row 1 of Plait Cable, p1 (2, 2, 2, 2, 2, 3, 3, 4), work Row 1 of Diamond Cable, p1 (2, 2, 2, 2, 2, 3, 3, 4), work Row 1 of Plait Cable, p1 (3, 7, 11, 2, 2, 3, 3, 4), work Row 1 of Plait Cable 0 (0, 0, 0, 1, 1, 1, 1, 1) time(s), p0 (0, 0, 0, 4, 9, 10, 13, 16), SM, p1 (3, 7, 11, 4, 9, 10, 14, 16), work Row 1 of Plait Cable 0 (0, 0, 0, 1, 1, 1, 1, 1) time(s), p1 (2, 2, 2, 2, 2, 3, 3, 4), work Row 1 of Diamond Cable, p1 (2, 2, 2, 2, 2, 3, 3, 4), work Row 1 of Plait Cable, p1 (2, 2, 2, 2, 3, 3, 4), k2, p4, k2.

Cont in pat as set, following the Diamond Cable and Plait Cable patterns, until you complete Row 14 of the Diamond Cable.

For the next 6 rows, you will create a Garter Stitch edging for what will become the pocket openings in the first and last Diamond Cables only. The WS rows do not change, and on each RS row you will perform the C3BP and C3FP cables as usual, but will knit the sts in the center of the diamond instead of purling them. See Chart #2 for reference.

Working in pat as set for the rest of the piece and creating garter stitch pocket edging in first and last Diamond Cables, cont until you complete Row 20 of the Diamond Cable.

Next row (RS): Create pocket opening: Work to first Diamond Cable, *k2, BO 13 sts knitwise, place st currently on right-hand needle onto left, k2tog, k1, work to last Diamond Cable (on Left Front), rep from *, then work to end.

Next row (WS): Work to first Diamond Cable, *p2, CO 14 sts using Backwards Loop method, p2, work to last Diamond Cable (on Right Front), rep from *, then work to end.

Work in pat as set, creating buttonholes where necessary, until you have completed Rows 1-36 of the Diamond Cable a total of 3 times, ending with a WS row.

Split Fronts and Back:

Work in pat to 1 (2, 3, 4, 4, 5, 5, 6, 6) st(s) past first marker, removing marker as you come to it, place last 2 (4, 6, 8, 8, 10, 10, 12, 12) sts on hold for right underarm, work to 1 (2, 3, 4, 4, 5, 5, 6, 6) st(s) past second marker, removing marker as you come to it, place last 2 (4, 6, 8, 8, 10, 10, 12, 12) sts on hold for left underarm, then work to end. Turn work and cont with Left Front only.

Left Front

Armhole Shaping

Next Row (WS): Work to last 3 sts in pat as set, k2tog (k2tog, k2tog, k2tog, p2tog, p2tog, p2tog, p2tog, p2tog), p1 – 1 st dec.

From this point forward, you will work the st at the edge of the armhole in St st, knitting it on each RS row and purling it on each WS row.

Note: For sizes 52.5 - 64.25" you will begin to shape the front neckline before the armhole shaping is complete. Please read through the entire Left Front section before proceeding, as you will have two sets of shaping going on at the same time.

Armhole Dec Row (RS): K1, p2tog (p2tog, p2tog, p2tog, ssk, ssk, ssk, ssk, ssk), work to end in pat as set – 1 st dec.

Working in pat as set, rep Armhole Dec Row every RS row 3 (3, 3, 4, 5, 8, 11, 11, 16) more times, then every 4th row 0 (1, 2, 3, 4, 4, 4, 5, 4) time(s).

Note: For sizes 47.75 to 64.25", the armhole decreases will travel through and eliminate the Plait Cable closest to the armhole edge. When there are not enough sts to complete either the C6F or the C6B, simply work the sts in St st. Also note that for all sizes but 52.5", 60", and 64.25", the armhole decreases will reduce the number of sts available for the Diamond Cable from 18 to 12 (12, 14, 15, 17, -, 17, -, -). The left "k2" side of the diamond may be worked as usual. But, when there is only 1 st rem to the right of the right "k2" side of the diamond, work the 3 sts at the armhole edge in St st until you are at the point in the second half of the diamond where the the "k2" is in the same position (e.g. Refer to Chart #2 – the "k2's" are in the same position in Row 11 and Row 33) and you can move it away from the edge again with C4F.

Sizes 32.25 (36, 39.75, 44, 47.75, -, -, -, -)" ONLY:

After last Armhole Dec is complete, work 12 (10, 6, 2, 0, -, -, -, -) rows in pat as set, then cont to Neck Edge Shaping.

Sizes - (-, -, -, -, 52.5 55.75, 60, 64.25)" ONLY:

AT THE SAME TIME, when you have 18 (20, 22, 24, 28, 32, 35, 37,

41) sts for the Left Front, work - (-, -, -, -, 2, 2, 2, 0) rows in pat as set, then cont to Neck Edge shaping.

Neck Edge Shaping

Next Row (WS): BO 11 (12, 13, 14, 14, 14, 14, 15, 15), work to last st in pat, p1.

Neck Edge Dec Row (RS): Work to last 3 sts in pat as set, k2tog, k1 – 1 st dec.

From this point forward, you will work the st at the neck edge in St st, knitting it on each RS row and purling it on each WS row. As before, when there are not enough sts to complete the C6F or C6B of the Plait Cable, simply work the rem sts in St st.

Working in pat as set, and incorporating Armhole Shaping as necessary for sizes 52.5 - 64.25", rep Neck Edge Dec Row every RS row 7 (7, 6, 8, 8, 7, 7, 9, 8) more times, then every 4th row 0 (0, 1, 0, 0, 1, 1, 0, 1) time(s). 13 (14, 15, 15, 17, 18, 18, 19, 19) sts.

Work 1 WS row in pat, then BO all sts.

Right Front

Rejoin yarn at WS of Right Front.

Armhole Shaping

Next Row (WS): P1, ssk (ssk, ssk, ssk, ssp, ssp, ssp, ssp, ssp), work to end in pat as set – 1 st dec.

From this point forward, you will work the st at the edge of the armhole in St st, knitting it on each RS row and purling it on each WS row.

Note: For sizes 47.75 - 64.25" you will begin to shape the front neckline before the armhole shaping is complete. Please read through the entire Right Front section before proceeding, as you will have two sets of shaping going on at the same time.

Armhole Dec Row (RS): Incorporating buttonholes where necessary, work to last 3 sts in pat as set, p2tog (p2tog, p2tog, k2tog, k2tog, k2tog, k2tog, k2tog), k1 – 1 st dec.

Working in pat as set, rep Armhole Dec Row every RS row 3 (3, 3, 4, 5, 8, 11, 11, 16) more times, then every 4th row 0 (1, 2, 3, 4, 4, 4, 5, 4) time(s).

Note: In the Left Front section regarding decreasing through the Plait Cable and Diamond Cable. The same instructions apply, but the left "k2" side of the diamond in the Diamond Cable is the side closest to the armhole.

Sizes 32.25 (36, 39.75, 44, -, -, -, -, -)" ONLY:

After last Armhole Dec is complete, work 11 (9, 5, 1, -, -, -, -, -) row(s) in pat as set, then cont to Neck Edge Shaping.

Size 47.75" ONLY:

Begin Neck Edge Shaping on THE SAME ROW as your last Armhole Dec Row.

Sizes – (-, -, -, -, 52.5 55.75, 60, 64.25)" ONLY:

AT THE SAME TIME, when you have - (-, -, -, -, 32, 35, 37, 42) sts for the Right Front, work 1 row in pat as set, then cont to Neck Edge shaping.

Neck Edge Shaping

Next Row (RS): BO 10 (11, 12, 13, 13, 13, 13, 14, 14), work to last st in pat, k1.

Next Row (WS): Work in pat as set to last 3 sts, ssp, p1 – 1 st dec.

Neck Edge Dec Row (RS): K1, ssk, work to end in pat as set – 1 st dec.

From this point forward, you will work the st at the neck edge in St st, knitting it on each RS row and purling it on each WS row. As before, when there are not enough sts to complete the C6F or C6B of the Plait Cable, simply work the remaining sts in St st.

Working in pat as set, and incorporating Armhole Shaping as necessary for sizes 52.5 - 64.25", rep Neck Edge Dec Row every RS row 7 (7, 6, 8, 8, 7, 7, 9, 8) more times, then every 4th row 0 (0, 1, 0, 0, 1, 1, 0, 1) time(s). 13 (14, 15, 15, 17, 18, 18, 19, 19) sts.

Work 1 WS row in pat, then BO all sts.

Back

Rejoin yarn at WS of Back.

Next row (WS): P1, p2tog (p2tog, p2tog, p2tog, ssk, ssk, ssk, ssk, ssk), work to last 3 sts in pat as set, p2tog (p2tog, p2tog, p2tog, k2tog, k2tog, k2tog, k2tog, k2tog), p1 – 2 sts dec.

From this point forward, you will work the sts at the edges of the armhole in St st, knitting them on each RS row and purling them on each WS row.

Armhole Dec Row (RS): K1, ssk (ssk, ssk, ssk, ssp, ssp, ssp, ssp, ssp), work to last 3 sts in pat as set, k2tog (k2tog, k2tog, k2tog, p2tog, p2tog, p2tog, p2tog, p2tog), k1 – 2 sts dec.

Working in pat as set, rep Armhole Dec Row every RS row 3 (3, 3, 4, 5, 8, 11, 11, 16) more times, then every 4th row 0 (1, 2, 3, 4, 4, 4, 5, 4) time(s). 57 (61, 65, 67, 71, 73, 75, 79, 81) sts.

Note: For all sizes except 52.5", 60", and 64.25", the armhole decreases will reduce the sts available for the applicable Plait Cables from 9 to 3 (2, 5, 6, 7, -, 7, -, -). For the sizes with fewer than 6 sts available, simply work the first and last 4 (3, 6, -, -, -, -, -, -) sts in St st at the Armhole edges. For the sizes with 6 or more sts remaining for the Plait Cables, you may continue to work C6B (Plait Cable Row 5) on the right armhole edge and C6F (Plait Cable Row 1) on the left armhole edge.

Work in pat as set for 29 (27, 25, 21, 19, 15, 11, 11, 7) more rows, or until armhole measures the same as the Left and Right Fronts, ending with a WS row.

BO all sts.

Sleeves

Seam Left Front and Right Front to Back at shoulders.

Using US 9 (5.5mm) needles preferred for working sleeves in the round, place 2 (4, 8, 8, 10, 10, 12, 12) held underarm sts on needle, then beg just to the left of the held underarm sts, pick up 35 (38, 41, 42, 46, 49, 51, 54, 56) sts up armhole edge to shoulder seam and 35 (38, 41, 42, 46, 49, 51, 54, 56) more sts down armhole edge to underarm. 72 (80, 88, 92, 100, 108, 112, 120, 124) sts.

Next Rnd: P1 (2, 3, 4, 4, 5, 5, 6, 6), then PM to mark beg of rnd.

Next Rnd: Beg sleeve ribbing: *K2, p2, rep from * to end. Rep last rnd 1 time.

Short Row 1 (RS): Work in 2x2 ribbing as set to 4 (6, 8, 10, 10, 12, 12, 14, 14) sts from end of rnd, w&t.

Short Row 2 (WS): Rep Short Row #1.

Short Row 3: Work in 2x2 ribbing to 2 sts from last wrap, w&t. Rep Short Row 3 13 (15, 17, 17, 21, 23, 25, 27, 29) more times.

After last w&t, work in 2x2 ribbing to end of rnd, incorporating wraps with their associated sts.

Next Rnd: Work in 2x2 ribbing to end, incorporating remaining wraps with their associated sts.

Dec for Upper Arm: [K2tog, p2] 2 (1, 2, 3, 3, 3, 4, 4, 4) time(s), [k2tog, p2tog] to last 8 (4, 8, 12, 12, 12, 16, 16, 16) sts, [k2tog, p2] 2 (1, 2, 3, 3, 3, 4, 4, 4) time(s) – 40 (42, 48, 52, 56, 60, 64, 68, 70) sts.

Work in pat as set, knitting all k sts and purling all p sts, for 2 (2, 2, 3, 3, 3, 4, 4, 4) rnds.

BO all sts in pat.

Collar

Using US 9 (5.5 mm) circular needles and starting at the Right Front edge, pick up 10 (11, 12, 13, 13, 13, 13, 14, 14) sts from the BO neck edge, roughly 4 sts for every 5 rows up to the right shoulder, 31 (33, 35, 37, 37, 37, 39, 41, 43) sts from the BO back neck edge, roughly 4 sts for every 5 rows down from the left shoulder, then 10 (11, 12, 13, 13, 13, 13, 14, 14) sts from the BO Left Front neck edge – 82 (86, 94, 98, 98, 98, 102, 106, 110) sts.

Note: The exact number of sts is not important, so long as you have a multiple of 4 sts plus 2.

Next row (WS): P2, k4, p2, *k2, p2; rep from * to last 6 sts, k4, p2.

Note: The first and last 8 sts continue the button band pat.

Cont in pat as set until collar measures 3.5" slightly stretched. BO all sts in pat.

Pocket Linings

With bottom of sweater toward you and WS facing up, pick up 1 st to right of BO pocket opening, 14 sts from BO edge of pocket opening, and 1 st to the left – 16 sts. Beg with a k row, work 22 rows in Reverse St st. Do not BO. Break yarn and sew down live sts of pocket lining to last row of ribbing.

Finishing

Seam sides of pocket linings to Body.

Weave in ends, wash and block to measurements in diagram.

Sew buttons to left side button band at same intervals as buttonholes.

Chart #1: Plait Cable

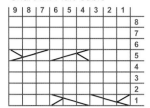

Chart #2: Diamond Cable

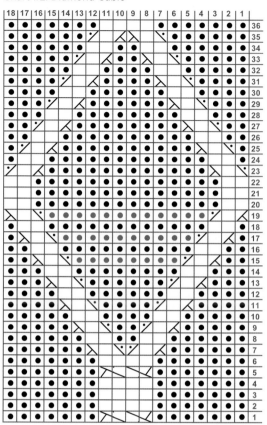

Legend:

⊡	**purl**	purl stitch
	c2 over 2 left	sl 2 to CN, hold in front. k2, k2 from CN
☐	**knit**	knit stitch
	c2 over 1 right P	sl1 to CN, hold in back. k2, p1 from CN
	c2 over 1 left P	sl2 to CN, hold in front. p1, k2 from CN
	c3 over 3 left	sl3 to CN, hold in front. k3, k3 from CN
	c3 over 3 right	sl3 to CN, hold in back. k3, then k3 from CN

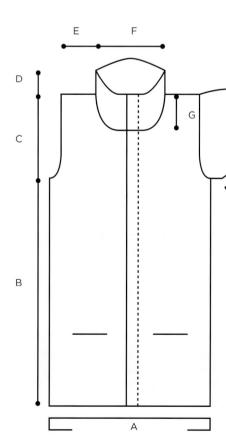

A 32.25 (36, 39.75, 44, 44.75, 52.5, 55.75, 60, 64.25)"
B 23.75"
C 7.25 (7.5, 8, 8.5, 9.25, 9.5, 10, 10.75, 11)"
D 3.5"
E 3 (3.25, 3.5, 3.5, 4, 4.25, 4.25, 4.5, 4.5)"
F 7.25 (7.75, 8.25, 8.75, 8.75, 8.75, 9.25, 9.75, 10)"
G 3.5 (3.5, 3.75, 3.75, 3.75, 4.25, 4.25, 4.25, 4.5)"
H 11.5 (12, 13.75, 14.75, 16, 17.25, 18.25, 19.5, 20)"

JAYASHRI

by Meghan Jones

FINISHED MEASUREMENTS

34 (38, 42, 46, 50, 54, 58, 62)" finished bust measurement; garment is meant to be worn with 2" positive ease.

YARN

MC: Knit Picks Gloss DK (70% Merino Wool, 30% Silk; 123 yards/50g): Fedora 24723: 8 (9 ,10, 11, 12, 13, 15, 16) balls

CC: Knit Picks Palette (100% Peruvian Highland Wool; 231 yards/50g): Puma Heather 26059: 1 ball.

NEEDLES

US 5 (3.75mm) 32" (largest sizes may need a 47") circular needles, or size to obtain gauge

US 6 (4mm) 32" (largest sizes may need a 47") circular needles, or size to obtain gauge

US 6 (4mm) set of 4 DPNs, or size to obtain gauge

NOTIONS

Yarn Needle
Stitch Markers
Cable needles
Scrap yarn or stitch holder
3 buttons, optional

GAUGE

22 sts and 28 rows = 4" in Stockinette st, using US6 (4mm) needles

Jayashri

Notes:

The Jayashri sweater is worked in one piece from the bottom up in the round. Yoke is shaped using raglan decreases. Sleeves are worked bottom-up in the round, and then seamed to the body. This pattern includes optional short row bust shaping to add 0.75 (1, 1.5)" of length to the front of the garment.

Notes on Sizing: Throughout this pattern there are notes made on how to rework increases or decreases if you are altering the pattern sizing. Please note that any changes to the number of increases or decreases will alter the finished garment so it will no longer match the included schematic or measurements. It is highly recommended to sit down with the pattern and work out all adjustments according to the body measurements desired before beginning to work the pattern.

Garter Stitch (worked in the round over any number of sts)
Rnd 1: P around
Rnd 2: K around

Garter Slip Stitch (worked flat over 7sts)
Row 1: P3, Sl1 kwise wyib, P3
Row 2: P7

Garter Slip Stitch (worked in the round over 7sts)
Rnd 1: P3, Sl1 kwise wyib, P3
Rnd 2: K7

Left Front Garter Slip Stitch (worked flat over 7sts)
Row 1: K3, Sl1 kwise wyib, K3
Row 2: K3, P1, K3

Pleating Stitch (worked in the round over 9 sts)
Turn work to the WS. With active stitches facing down, using spare DPN count down 8 rows from the top, (8 purl stitches or bumps) place 8th bump counted from the top onto the DPN, working from right to left place the following 8 stitches in the same row 8 rows down from the active row onto the DPN. The 9 sts that are placed onto the DPN correspond to the 9 sts between the markers but are 8 rows below them on the WS. Turn work back to the RS to work across active stitches, fold work so that stitches on DPN are directly behind 9 active stitches between markers.

Row 1: *Insert right needle tip into first stitch on needle and 1st held stitch on DPN, k2tog; rep from * for remaining 8 sts.

DIRECTIONS
Main Body

Using smaller needles and MC, cast on 204 (226, 248, 270, 292, 314, 336, 358) sts, join to work in the round being careful not to twist. PM to indicate beginning of round.

Work Garter Stitch in the round for 16 rnds, or until piece measures approx 1.75" from cast on edge.

Change to larger needles.

Setup Rnd: *K24 (27, 30, 32, 36, 39, 42, 44), PM, work Garter Slip Stitch (worked in the round) over following 7 sts, PM, K40 (45, 50, 57, 60, 65, 70, 77) sts, PM, work Garter Slip Stitch (worked in the round) over following 7 sts, K24 (27, 30, 32, 36, 39, 42, 44), PM; rep from * once more, last PM will be beginning of rnd marker.

Work evenly in St st and Garter Slip Stitch pattern as established until piece measures 2.25 (2.25, 2.25, 2.25, 2.75, 2.75, 2.75, 2.75)" from cast on edge.

Note on Sizing: If you are adjusting length, this is the area to add or remove length. Make sure to add or subtract the difference in length for all following length measurements.

If you are adjusting circumference, each decrease uses 0.5" of length and reduces the circumference by 0.75". If you are working fewer decreases to create a larger waist circumference, you need to work an additional 0.5" before beginning the decreases. Likewise, if you are working more decreases for a smaller waist circumference, you need to work 0.5" less before beginning decreases.

Dec Rnd: *Work in pattern to 3 sts before m, Ssk, K1, SM, work to 3rd marker from needle, SM, K1, K2tog, K to marker, SM; rep from * once more. – 200 (222, 244, 266, 288, 310, 332, 354) sts

Continuing in pattern, rep Dec Rnd every 4 rnds 6 more times. – 176 (198, 220, 242, 264, 286, 308, 330) sts

Work evenly in pattern until piece measures 10 (9.5, 10, 9.5, 9.5, 9, 9.25, 9)" from cast on edge.

Note on Sizing: If you are working more increases to enlarge the bust circumference, remove 2 even rounds from the repeat for every increase you add. If you are working fewer increases to decrease the bust size, the first increase round should still be worked at the indicated measurement in the pattern.

Inc Rnd: *Work in pattern to 1 st before marker, M1R, K1, SM, work to 3rd marker from needle, SM, K1, M1L, work to marker, SM; rep from * once more. – 180 (202, 224, 246, 268, 290, 312, 334) sts

Continuing in pattern, rep Inc Rnd every 6 rnds 2 times more. – 188 (210, 232, 254, 276, 298, 320, 342) sts

Work evenly in pattern until piece measures 15 (15, 15.5, 15.5, 16, 16, 16.5, 16.5)" from cast on edge.

Optional Short Rows (to add 0.75 (1, 1.25)" of length to the front):

Short Row 1 (RS): Work to 1 st before 5th marker, w&t
Short Row 2 (WS): Work to 1 st before beginning of rnd marker, w&t
Short Row 3: Work to 2 sts before last wrapped stitch, w&t
Rep last row 1 (3, 5) times

Resume working in the round, continuing Garter Slip Stitch pattern. Work in set of wraps on the Right side of body on this rnd. Work in second set of wraps on the Left side of body when working the armhole shaping on the next rnd.

Armhole Shaping: *K to 5 (5, 6, 6, 7, 7, 8, 8) sts before 5th marker, BO 10 (10, 12, 12, 14, 14, 16, 16) sts and remove marker; rep from * once more, last marker removed is beginning of round marker. – 168 (190, 208, 230, 248, 270, 288, 310) sts total, 84 (95, 104, 115,

124, 135, 144, 155) sts each on front and back.

Place all stitches onto holder or waste yarn.

Sleeves (make 2)

Using smaller needles and MC, cast on 58 (64, 72, 77, 87, 94, 100, 108) sts, leaving a 6" tail. Join to work in the round being careful not to twist, PM to indicate beginning of round.

Work Garter Stitch in the round for 16 rnds, or until piece measures approx 1.75" from cast on edge.

Change to larger needles.

Next Rnd: K around.
Inc Rnd: K1, M1L, K to last stitch, M1R, K1

Continuing in pattern, rep Inc Rnd every 6 rnds 2 times more. – 64 (70, 78, 83, 93, 100, 106, 114) sts

If necessary, work evenly until piece measures 5" from cast on edge.

Armhole Shaping: K to last 5 (5, 6, 6, 7, 7, 8, 8) sts, BO 10 (10, 12, 12, 14, 14, 16, 16) sts removing marker. – 54 (60, 66, 71, 79, 86, 90, 98) sts.

Raglan Yoke

Reattach yarn to work RS of Main body front. If you worked the optional short rows, this is the side the short rows were worked on; if you didn't work short rows either side can be the front. All markers placed in the following Setup Rnd will be referred to as Raglan markers from now on, remaining markers that indicate Garter Slip Stitch patterning should remain in the work until those stitches are used by the Raglan decreases.

Setup Rnd: Continuing in pattern as established, work across front to armhole opening, PM, work across RS of sleeve in St st to armhole opening, PM, work across back to armhole opening, PM, work across RS of sleeve in St st to armhole opening, PM to indicate beg of rnd. – 276 (310, 340, 372, 406, 442, 468, 506) sts

Sizes 34 (38, 42, 46) only:

Work evenly in pattern as established until piece measures 2 (2, 1.5, 0.5)" from Setup Rnd.

All Sizes:
Raglan Shaping Rnd: *K1, K2tog, work to 3 sts before raglan marker, Ssk, k1, SM; Rep from * 3 more times. – 268 (302, 332, 364, 398, 434, 460, 498) sts.

Continuing in pattern, rep Raglan Shaping Rnd every 2 rnds 10 (13, 16, 19, 23, 27, 29, 33) times. – 188 (198, 204, 212, 214, 218, 228, 234) sts.

Front Neck Shaping:
Work evenly in pattern (do not work first raglan decrease) to marker before center St st section (this was the 2nd marker in the Main Body but may have been removed during Raglan Shaping), SM, K17 (18, 19, 21, 21, 22, 23, 25), BO 10 (13, 16, 19, 18, 21, 24, 27) sts. – 178 (185, 188, 193, 196, 197, 204, 207) sts.

The remaining stitches are worked back and forth. Raglan decreases are continued on the RS of the work while the WS is

worked even. The Garter Slip Stitch pattern on the left front of the main body is now worked as Front Left Garter Slip Stitch.

Row 1 (RS): Continuing all Raglan decreases and Garter Slip Stitch patterns as established, work to end of row. –170 (177, 180, 185, 188, 189, 196, 199) sts.
Row 2 (WS): Work evenly in pattern as established.

Working in pattern and continuing Raglan decreases on the RS rows, BO 3 (3, 3, 4, 4, 4, 4, 4) sts at beginning of each of next 6 rows. –128 (135, 138, 137, 140, 141, 148, 151) sts.

Working in pattern and continuing Raglan decreases on the RS rows, BO 2 sts at beginning of each of next 6 rows. –92 (99, 102, 101, 104, 105, 112, 115) sts.

Short Row 1 (RS): Work evenly in pattern to 3 sts before 2nd Raglan marker (Right Back) Ssk, K1, SM, K1, K2tog, work to 3 sts before 3rd Raglan marker (Left Back) Ssk, K1, SM, K1, K2tog, K to 4 sts before last Raglan marker (Left Front), w&t. – 88 (95, 98, 97, 100, 101, 108, 111) sts.
Short Row 2 (WS): Work in pattern to 4 sts before last Raglan marker (Right Front), w&t
Short Row 3: Continuing decreases as in Short Row 1, work to 2 sts before last wrapped stitch, w&t. – 84 (91, 94, 93, 96, 97, 104, 107) sts.
Short Row 4: Work in pattern to 2 sts before last wrapped stitch, w&t.
Short Row 5: Continuing decreases as in Short Rows 1 and 3 work in pattern to end of row working in wraps. – 80 (87, 90, 89, 92, 93, 100, 103) sts.
Short Row 6: P2tog, work to end working in wraps. – 79 (86, 89, 88, 91, 92, 99, 102) sts.

BO all stitches, beginning with an Ssk.

Collar

Using smaller needles and MC and beginning at Right Back raglan decrease, pickup and knit 42 (47, 50, 55, 56, 59, 64, 67) sts across back neck to next raglan decrease, 6 (6, 6, 5, 5, 4, 4, 4) sts to middle of sleeve, PM, 9 sts to Left Front raglan decrease, PM, 48 (53, 56, 61, 62, 65, 70, 73) sts across front to Right Front raglan decrease, PM, 9 sts across sleeve, PM, 6 (6, 6, 5, 5, 4, 4, 4) sts to Right Back raglan decrease, PM for beginning of rnd. –120 (130, 136, 144, 146, 150, 157, 166) sts.

Work Garter Stitch in the round for 3 rounds.

Change to CC and larger needles.

Next Rnd: K around.
Inc Rnd: *K3, M1L; rep from * 15 (16, 17, 19, 19, 21, 22, 23) times, K to marker (if necessary), **K3, M1L; rep from ** 17 (18, 19, 21, 21, 22, 23, 24) times, K to end of rnd (if necessary). – 154 (166, 174, 186, 188, 192, 204, 215) sts.

Work St st in the round for 1.5".

Place removable marker to indicate first stitch of next rnd.

Work St st in the round for 8 rounds.

Pleating Rnd: *K to m, SM, working Pleating Stitch across 9 sts, SM; Rep from * once more, K to end.

Working in St st, rep Pleating Rnd every 9 rnds twice more.

Next Rnd: K around.
Dec Rnd: *K2, K2tog; rep from * 15 (16, 17, 19, 19, 21, 22) times, K to marker, **K2, K2tog; rep from ** 17 (18, 19, 21, 21, 22, 23, 24) times, K to end of rnd. – 120 (130, 136, 144, 146, 150, 157, 166) sts.

BO all stitches, leaving a tail twice as long as the circumference of the neckline. Using Tapestry needle, sew bound off edge of collar to color change from MC to CC on inside of garment.

Tabs (make 3)
Using DPNS and MC, cast on 16 sts, leaving a 10" tail for seaming. Join to work in the round being careful not to twist, PM to indicate beginning of round.

Rnd 1: *Sl1, K7; rep from * once more.
Rnd 2: K around.
Rep Rnds 1-2 until piece measures 4" from cast on edge.

Dec Rnd 1: *Sl1, Ssk, K3, K2tog; rep from * once more. – 12 sts
Dec Rnd 2: K around.
Dec Rnd 3: *Sl1, Ssk, K1, K2tog; rep from * once more. – 8 sts
Dec Rnd 4: K around.
Dec Rnd 5: *Sl1, Sl1 k2tog psso; rep from * once more. – 4sts

Cut yarn, using tapestry needle thread through all stitches and fasten off, work in this end only.

Finishing
Using Tapestry needle, seam underarms with tails left from Sleeve armhole shaping.

With RS facing, fold bottom of sleeve outward and tack in place using tail from Sleeve cast on. Lay garment flat to determine exact top of sleeve. With bottom cuff of sleeve folded RS facing as at underarm, attach tab as follows. Place tab on inside of sleeve with edge aligned to top of cuff folded on the outside of sleeve, using tapestry needle and tail left from Tab cast on stitch through the tab cast on, sleeve, and cuff top, then back down through cuff top, sleeve and tab cast on. In this manner attach all of Tab cast on to sleeve and cuff. Fold Tabs to outside of sleeve around cuff and attach by sewing button in center of Tab using sewing needle and thread. Repeat for other sleeve tab.

Either wet block or steam collar to fold down onto outside of garment and lie flat. Arrange Neckline Tab on the left front of the garment, off center and on the inside neckline. Using Tapestry needle and tail left from cast on attach tab cast on to inner neck along seam from collar.

Using Tapestry needle, work in any loose ends.

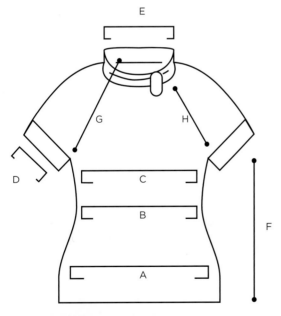

A 37 (41, 45, 49, 53, 57, 61, 65)"
B 32 (36, 40, 44, 48, 52, 56, 60)"
C 34 (38, 42, 46, 50, 54, 58, 62)"
D 10.5 (11.5, 13, 14, 15.75, 17, 18.25, 19.5)"
E 21.75 (23.75, 24.75, 26, 26.5, 27.25, 28.5, 30)"
F 15 (15, 15.5, 15.5, 16, 16, 16.5, 16.5)"
G 7 (8, 8.25, 8.25, 8.75, 10, 10.5, 11.75)"
H 5 (6, 6.25, 6.25, 6.75, 8, 8.5, 9.75)"

Abbreviations	
Beg	Beginning
CC	Contrast color
DPN	Double-pointed needle
Kwise	Knit wise, as if to knit
MC	Main color
PM	Place marker
Rnd	Round
RS	Right side
Sl	Slip stitch
St st	Stockinette stitch
WS	Wrong Side
Wyib	With yarn in back of work
Wyif	With yarn in front of work

BELT CARDI

by Jenise Reid

FINISHED MEASUREMENTS

20 (24, 28, 32, 36, 40, 44)" finished waist measurement; garment is meant to be worn with no ease. If your waist is between sizes, knit the next size up and make the belt shorter.

YARN

Knit Picks Capra DK (85% Merino Wool, 15% Cashmere; 123 yards/50g): Timber 24964: 7 (7, 8, 9, 10, 11, 12) balls.

NEEDLES

US 5 (3.75mm) 36" or longer circular needle, or size to obtain gauge
US 5 (3.75mm) DPNs or two 24" circular needles for two circulars technique, or one 32" or longer circular needle for Magic Loop technique, or size to obtain gauge
Spare DPN, US 5 (3.75mm)

NOTIONS

Yarn Needle
Stitch Markers
Scrap yarn or stitch holder
One 2" button
Sewing Thread
Needle
Heavy duty stabilizer, oval approx 2x3"

GAUGE

18 sts and 28 rows = 4" over Stockinette stitch, blocked.

Belt Cardi

Notes:

This sweater is knit from the bottom up. The body is knit back and forth, and the sleeves are knit in the round up to the underarm. Then, the underarm from the sleeve is grafted to the underarm of the body, and the yoke is knit up from there. The border is knit along with the body, and once the yoke is completed, the border continues along the neckline. The belt is picked up and knit from the border. As long as you block the body first, you can try on the sweater as you knit the belt and customize the amount of ease on it. A button is sewed onto a heavy duty stabilizer instead of the knit fabric to avoid distortion of the fabric.

Special Stitches and Abbreviations:

LKI (Make 1 Left-leaning stitch):

PU the bar between st just worked and next st and place on LH needle as a regular stitch; knit through the back loop.

RKI (Make 1 Right-leaning stitch):

PU the bar between st just worked and next st and place on LH needle backwards (incorrect stitch mount). Knit through the front loop.

S4K:

Slip four stitches together as one, knit through the back loop. 3 sts dec.

5/5 LC:

Slip 5 stitches to cable needle and hold in front; [k1, p1] 2 times, k1; [k1, p1] 2 times, k1 from cable needle.

5/5 RC:

Slip 5 stitches to cable needle and hold in back; [k1, p1] 2 times, k1; [k1, p1] 2 times, k1 from cable needle.

DIRECTIONS

Body

Cast on 116 (134, 150, 168, 192, 210, 226) sts.

Note: Even numbered rows are RS rows, odd numbered rows are WS rows. To create a neat selvedge, slip the first stitch on WS rows with yarn in front, and on RS rows with yarn in back. Stitch markers are placed on Rows 1 and 2 to mark sections of the garment. On the following rows, slip markers as you come to them.

Row 1 (WS): Sl1 wyif, k 1 (1, 1, 1, 2, 2, 2), [p2, k1] 3 (3, 3, 3, 4, 4, 4) times, p2, k2, PM, [p3, k1] 21 (25, 29, 34, 38, 42, 46) times, p 2 (4, 4, 2, 2, 4, 4), PM, k2, [p2, k1] 3 (3, 3, 3, 4, 4, 4) times, p2, k1 (1, 1, 1, 2, 2, 2), p1.

Row 2 (RS): Sl1, k 3 (3, 3, 3, 4, 4, 4), p1, [k2, p1] 2 (2, 2, 2, 3, 3, 3) times, PM, k 6 (8, 8, 6, 6, 8, 8), [p1, k3] 20 (24, 28, 33, 37, 41, 45) times, p1, k7, PM, [p1, k2] 2 (2, 2, 2, 3, 3, 3) times, p1, k 4 (4, 4, 4, 5, 5, 5).

Rows 3-28: Repeat rows 1-2.

Row 29 (WS): Work in pat as est to 2nd marker, SM, p next marker, SM, work in pat as est to end.

Row 30 (RS): Work in pat as est to first marker, SM, k4, RKI, k 7 (11, 15, 19, 23, 27, 31), k2tog, k6, ssk, k 52 (62, 70, 80, 88, 98, 106), k2tog, k6, ssk, k 7 (11, 15, 19, 23, 27, 31), LKI, k4, SM, work in pat as est to end. 114 (132, 148, 166, 190, 208, 224) sts.

Row 31: Work in pat as est to 2nd marker, SM, p to next marker, SM, work in pat as est to end.

Row 32: Work in pat as est to first marker, SM , k to last marker, SM, work in pat as est to end.

Row 33: Rep Row 31.

Row 34: Work in pat as est to first marker, SM, k4, RKI, k 8 (12, 16, 20, 24, 28, 32), k2tog, k4, ssk, k 52 (62, 70, 80, 88, 98, 106), k2tog, k4, ssk, k 8 (12, 16, 20, 24, 28, 32), LKI, k4, SM, work in pat as est to end. 112 (130, 146, 164, 188, 206, 222) sts.

Rows 35-37: Rep Rows 31-32, then work Row 31 again.

Row 38: Work in pat as est to first marker, SM, k4, RKI, k 7 (11, 15, 19, 23, 27, 31), k2tog, k6, ssk, k 48 (58, 66, 76, 84, 94, 102), k2tog, k6, ssk, k 7 (11, 15, 19, 23, 27, 31), LKI, k4, SM, work in pat as est to end. 110 (128, 144, 162, 186, 204, 220) sts.

Rows 39-41: Rep Rows 31-32, then work Row 31 again.

Row 42: Work in pat as est to first marker, SM, k4, RKI, k 8 (12, 16, 20, 24, 28, 32), k2tog, k4, ssk, k 48 (58, 66, 76, 84, 94, 102), k2tog, k4, ssk, k 8 (12, 16, 20, 24, 28, 32), LKI, k4, SM, work in pat as est to end. 108 (126, 142, 160, 184, 202, 218) sts.

Rows 43-45: Rep Rows 31-32, then work Row 31 again.

Row 46: Work in pat as est to first marker, SM, k4, RKI, k 7 (11, 15, 19, 23, 27, 31), k2tog, k6, ssk, k 44 (54, 62, 72, 80, 90, 98), k2tog, k6, ssk, k 7 (11, 15, 19, 23, 27, 31), LKI, k4, SM, work in pat as est to end. 106 (124, 140, 158, 182, 200, 216) sts.

Rows 47-49: Rep Rows 31-32, then work Row 31 again.

Row 50: Work in pat as est to first marker, SM, k4, RKI, k 8 (12, 16, 20, 24, 28, 32), k2tog, k4, ssk, k 44 (54, 62, 72, 80, 90, 98), k2tog, k4, ssk, k 8 (12, 16, 20, 24, 28, 32), LKI, k4, k4, SM, work in pat as est to end. 104 (122, 138, 156, 180, 198, 214) sts.

Row 51: Rep Row 31.

Row 52: Work in pat as est to first marker, SM, k3, LKI, RKI, k to last marker, work in pat as est to end. 106 (124, 140, 158, 182, 200, 216) sts.

Row 53: Work in pat as est to 2nd marker, SM, p to 2 sts before 3rd marker, k2. 91 (109, 125, 143, 163, 181, 197) sts.

Remove marker, sl the next 15 (15, 15, 15, 19, 19, 19) sts onto a stitch holder. This will make the slit for the belt to pass through. These stitches will be joined to the sweater body on Row 87.

Row 54: K2, RKI, k 7 (11, 15, 19, 23, 27, 31), k2tog, k6, ssk, k 40 (50, 58, 68, 76, 86, 94), k2tog, k6, ssk, k 7 (11, 15, 19, 23, 27, 31), LKI, work in pat as est to end. 89 (107, 123, 141, 161, 179, 195) sts.

Row 55: Work in pat as est to 2nd marker, p to last 2 sts, k2.

Row 56: K to 2nd marker, SM, work in pat as est to end.

Row 57: Rep Row 55.

Row 58: K2, RKI, k 8 (12, 16, 20, 24, 28, 32), k2tog, k4, ssk, k 40 (50, 58, 68, 76, 86, 94), k2tog, k4, ssk, k 8 (12, 16, 20, 24, 28, 32), LKI, work in pat as est to end. 87 (105, 121, 139, 159, 177, 193) sts.

Rows 59-61: Rep Rows 55-56, then work Row 55 again.

Row 62: K2, RKI, k 7 (11, 15, 19, 23, 27, 31), k2tog, k6, ssk, k 36 (46, 54, 64, 72, 82, 90), k2tog, k6, ssk, k 7 (11, 15, 19, 23, 27, 31), LKI, work in pat as est to end. 85 (103, 119, 137, 157, 175, 191) sts.

Rows 63-77: Rep Rows 55-56 seven times, then work Row 55 again.

Row 78: K 11 (15, 19, 23, 27, 31, 35), RKI, k6, LKI, k 38 (48, 56, 66, 74,

84, 92), RKI, k6, LKI, k 13 (17, 21, 25, 29, 33, 37), work in pat as est to end. 89 (107, 123, 141, 161, 179, 195) sts.

Rows 79-83: Rep Rows 55-56 two times, then work Row 55 again.

Row 84: K2, k2tog 0 (0, 0, 1, 1, 0, 0), K 11 (15, 19, 21, 25, 31, 35), RKI, k4, LKI, k 42 (52, 60, 70, 78, 88, 96), RKI, k4, LKI, k 11 (15, 19, 21, 25, 31, 35), ssk 0 (0, 0, 1, 1, 0, 0), k4, work in pat as est to end. 93 (111, 127, 143, 163, 183, 199) sts.

Rows 85-86: Rep Rows 55-56.

Place the 15 (15, 15, 15, 19, 19, 19) sts held on Row 53 back on needles. Join a new ball of yarn and work Extended Border over these held sts only.

Extended border:

Row 1: K2, [p2, k1] 3 (3, 3, 3, 4, 4, 4) times, p2, k 1 (1, 1, 1, 2, 2, 2), p1.

Row 2: Sl1, k 3 (3, 3, 3, 4, 4, 4), p1, [k2, p1] 2, (2, 2, 2, 3, 3, 3) times, k4.

Rows 3-34: Repeat rows 1-2.

Slide all the extended border stitches onto the opposite end of the needle so that row 87 will knit across the stitches used in row 86 and then continue onto the extended border section.

Row 87: Work in pat as est to 2nd marker, SM, ssp 1 (0, 0, 0, 0, 0, 0), p 72 (94, 110, 126, 142, 162, 178), p2tog 1 (0, 0, 0, 0, 0, 0), PM, k1, k3tog, [p2, k1] 3 (3, 3, 3, 4, 4, 4) times, p2, k1 (1, 1, 1, 2, 2, 2), p1. 104 (124, 140, 156, 180, 200, 216) sts.

Row 88: Sl1, k 3 (3, 3, 3, 4, 4, 4), p1, [k2, p1] 2 (2, 2, 2, 3, 3, 3) times, PM, k4, k2tog 0 (0, 0, 0, 1, 0, 1), k 74 (94, 110, 126, 138, 162, 174), ssk 0 (0, 0, 0, 1, 0, 1), k4, work in pat as est to end. 104 (124, 140, 156, 178, 200, 214) sts.

Row 89: Work in pat as est to 2nd marker, SM, ssp 0 (0, 0, 1, 0, 0, 0), p 74 (94, 110, 122, 140, 162, 176), p2tog 0 (0, 0, 1, 0, 0, 0), work in pat as est to end. 104 (124, 140, 154, 178, 200, 214) sts.

Row 90: Work in pat as est to first marker, SM, k 14 (19, 23, 25, 29, 35, 38), RKI, k6, LKI, k 42 (52, 60, 70, 78, 88, 96), RKI, k6, LKI, k 14 (19, 23, 25, 29, 35, 38), work in pat as est to end. 108 (128, 144, 158, 182, 204, 218) sts.

Row 91: Work in pat as est to 2nd marker, SM, ssp 0 (1, 1, 0, 0, 1, 0), p 78 (94, 110, 128, 144, 162, 176), p2tog 0 (1, 1, 0, 0, 1, 1), work in pat as est to end. 108 (126, 142, 158, 182, 202, 216) sts.

Row 92: Work in pat as est to first marker, SM, k4, k2tog 0 (0, 0,

0, 1, 0, 0), k 78 (96, 112, 128, 140, 164, 178), ssk 0 (0, 0, 0, 1, 0, 0), k4, work in pat as est to end. 108 (126, 142, 158, 180, 202, 216) sts.

Row 93: Work in pat as est to 2nd marker, SM, p to next marker, SM, work in pat as est to end.

Row 94: Work in pat as est to first marker, SM, k4, k2tog 0 (0, 0, 1, 0, 0, 1), k 78 (96, 112, 124, 142, 164, 174), ssk 0 (0, 0, 1, 0, 0, 1), k4, work in pat as est to end. 108 (126, 142, 156, 180, 202, 214) sts.

Row 95: Rep Row 93.

Row 96: Work in pat as est to first marker, SM, k4, k2tog 0 (0, 1, 0, 1, 1, 0), k 12 (16, 18, 22, 24, 30, 34), RKI, k4, LKI, k 46 (56, 64, 74, 82, 92, 100), RKI, k4, LKI, k 12 (16, 18, 22, 24, 30, 34), ssk 0 (0, 1, 0, 1, 1, 0), k4, work in pat as est to end. 112 (130, 144, 160, 182, 204, 218) sts.

Row 97: Work in pat as est to 2nd marker, SM, ssp 1 (0, 0, 0, 0, 0, 1), p 78 (100, 114, 130, 144, 166, 176), p2tog 1 (0, 0, 0, 0, 0, 1), work in pat as est to(0, 0, 0, 1, 1, 1), k 80 (98, 114, 128, 140, 162, 174), ssk 0 (0, 0, 0, 1, 1, 1), k4, work in pat as est to end. 110 (128, 144, 158, 180, 202, 214) sts.

Row 101: Work in pat as est to 2nd marker, SM, ssp 0 (0, 1, 0, 0, 0, 0), p 80 (98, 110, 128, 142, 164, 176), p2tog 0 (0, 1, 0, 0, 0, 0), work in pat as est to end. 110 (128, 142, 158, 180, 202, 214) sts.

Row 102: Work in pat as est to first marker, SM, k 15 (19, 22, 25, 28, 34, 36), RKI, k6, LKI, k 46 (56, 64, 74, 82, 92, 100), RKI, k6, LKI, k 15 (19, 22, 25, 28, 34, 36), work in pat as est to end. 114 (132, 146, 162, 184, 206, 218) sts. end.110 (130, 144, 160, 182, 204, 216) sts.

Row 98: Work in pat as est to first marker, SM, k4, k2tog 0 (1, 0, 0, 0, 0, 0), k 80 (96, 114, 130, 144, 166, 178), ssk 0 (1, 0, 0, 0, 0, 0), k4, work in pat as est to end. 110 (128, 144, 160, 182, 204, 216) sts.

Row 99: Work in pat as est to 2nd marker, SM, ssp 0 (0, 0, 1, 0, 0, 0), p 80 (98, 114, 126, 144, 166, 178), p2tog 0 (0, 0, 1, 0, 0, 0), work in pat as est to end. 110 (128, 144, 158, 182, 204, 216) sts.

Row 100: Work in pat as est to first marker, SM, k4, k2tog 0

Row 103: Work in pat as est to 2nd marker, SM, ssp 0 (0, 0, 0, 0, 1, 1), p 84 (102, 116, 132, 146, 164, 176), p2tog 0 (0, 0, 0, 0, 1, 1), work in pat as est to end. 114 (132, 146, 162, 184, 204, 216) sts.

Row 104: Work in pat as est to first marker, SM, k4, k2tog 0 (0, 0, 1, 1, 0, 0), k 84 (102, 116, 128, 142, 166, 178), ssk 0 (0, 0, 1, 1, 0, 0), k4, work in pat as est to end. 114 (132, 146, 160, 182, 204, 216) sts.

Row 105: Work in pat as est to 2nd marker, SM, ssp 0 (1, 0, 0, 0, 0, 0), p 84 (98, 116, 130, 144, 166, 178), p2tog 0 (1, 0, 0, 0, 0, 0), work in pat as est to end. 114 (130, 146, 160, 182, 204, 216) sts.

Row 106: Work in pat as est to first marker, SM, k4, k2tog 0 (0, 1, 0, 0, 1, 1), k 84 (100, 112, 130, 144, 162, 174), ssk 0 (0, 1, 0, 0, 1, 1), k4, work in pat as est to end. 114 (130, 144, 160, 182, 202, 214) sts.

Row 107: Work in pat as est to 2nd marker, SM, p to next marker, SM, work in pat as est to end.

Row 108: Work in pat as est to first marker, SM, k4, k2tog 1 (0, 0, 0, 1, 0, 0), k 11 (16, 19, 22, 23, 30, 32), RKI, k4, LKI, k 50 (60, 68, 78, 86, 96, 104), RKI, k4, LKI, k 11 (16, 19, 22, 23, 30, 32), ssk 1 (0, 0, 0, 1, 0, 0), k4, work in pat as est to end. 116 (134, 148, 164, 184, 206, 214) sts.

Row 109: Work in pat as est to 2nd marker, SM, ssp 0 (0, 0, 1, 0, 1, 1), p 86 (104, 118, 130, 146, 164, 176), p2tog 0 (0, 0, 1, 0, 1, 1), work in pat as est to end. 116 (134, 148, 162, 184, 204, 216) sts.

Row 110: Work in pat as est to first marker, SM, k to last marker, SM, work in pat as est to end.

Row 111: Work in pat as est to 2nd marker, SM, ssp 0 (0, 1, 0, 0, 0, 0), p 86 (104, 114, 132, 146, 166, 178), p2tog 0 (0, 1, 0, 0, 0, 0), work in pat as est to end. 116 (134, 146, 162, 184, 204, 216) sts.

Row 112: Work in pat as est to first marker, SM, k4, k2tog 0 (1, 0, 0, 1, 1, 1), k 86 (100, 116, 132, 142, 162, 174), ssk 0 (1, 0, 0, 1, 1, 1), k4, work in pat as est to end. 116 (132, 146, 162, 182, 202, 214) sts.

Sleeves (make two)

Cast on 54 (60, 64, 68, 74, 80, 84) sts, PM, and join in the round, making sure that there is not a twist.

Rounds 1-28: K1, [p1, k4] 10 (11, 12, 13, 14, 15, 16) times, p1, k 2 (3, 2, 1, 2, 3, 2)
Rounds 29-70: K 54 (60, 64, 68, 74, 80, 84).

Do not bind off, but cut the yarn leaving a tail at least 2 yds long. The tail will be used for grafting only, the body yarn will purl the sleeve stitches onto the body before continuing on with the yoke.

Yoke

Here we join up the sleeves to the body. To do this, work up to where the underarm is on the body, graft the underarm stitches to the same number of stitches from one of the sleeves, (alternately, you can place the underarm stitches from the body and sleeve onto stitch holders and weave them as you finish the cardigan rather than in this round), work the rest of the stitches from the sleeve onto the body needle using the body yarn, work across the back, join the next underarm and sleeve identical to the first, and work to the other side of the front. Before you begin

Round 1, mark off the stitches to be grafted with safety pins.

Row 1: Using the body yarn of the body needle, work in body pat as est to 2nd marker, SM, p 10 (12, 15, 17, 18, 22, 24).

Weave the next 10 (12, 12, 14, 16, 18, 18) sts to the next 10 (12, 12, 14, 16, 18, 18) from one of the sleeves using the sleeve yarn.

Picking up the body yarn again, p 44 (48, 52, 54, 58, 62, 66) sts (the rest of the sleeve stitches) onto the body needle, then p 46 (54, 62, 70, 76, 84, 92) sts from the body. Weave the next 10 (12, 12, 14, 16, 18, 18) sts to the next 10 (12, 12, 14, 16, 18, 18) from the other sleeve using the sleeve yarn.

Picking up the body yarn again, p 44 (48, 52, 54, 58, 62, 66) sts (the rest of the sleeve stitches) onto the body needle, then work p 10 (12, 15, 17, 18, 22, 24), work in body pat as est to end. 184 (204, 226, 242, 266, 290, 310) sts.

Row 2: Work in pat as est to first marker, SM, k4, k2tog 0 (0, 0, 1, 0, 0, 0), k 154 (174, 196, 208, 228, 252, 272), ssk 0 (0, 0, 1, 0, 0, 0), k4, work in pat as est to end. 184 (204, 226, 240, 266, 290, 310) sts.

Row 3: Work in pat as est to 2nd marker, SM, p 9 (11, 14, 15, 17, 21, 23), k2, p 42 (46, 50, 52, 56, 60, 64), k2, p 44 (52, 60, 68, 74, 82, 90), k2, p 42 (46, 50, 52, 56, 60, 64), k2, p 9 (11, 14, 15, 17, 21, 23), work in pat as est to end.

Row 4: Work in pat as est to first marker, SM, k4, k2tog 0 (0, 1, 0, 1, 1), k 154 (174, 192, 210, 224, 248, 268), ssk 0 (0, 1, 0, 1, 1), k4, work in pat as est to end. 184 (204, 224, 240, 264, 288, 308) sts.

Row 5: Work in pat as est to 2nd marker, SM, p 9 (11, 13, 15, 16, 20, 22), k2, p 42 (46, 50, 52, 56, 60, 64), k2, p 44 (52, 60, 68, 74, 82, 90), k2, p 42 (46, 50, 52, 56, 60, 64), k2, p 9 (11, 13, 15, 16, 20, 22), work in pat as est to end.

Row 6: Work in pat as est to first marker, SM, k4, k 11 (13, 15, 17, 18, 22, 24), k2tog, k 38 (42, 46, 48, 52, 56, 60), ssk, k2, k2tog 0 (0, 0, 0, 1, 1), k 44 (52, 60, 68, 74, 78, 86), ssk 0 (0, 0, 0, 1, 1), k2, k2tog, k 38 (42, 46, 48, 52, 56, 60), ssk, k 11 (13, 15, 17, 18, 22, 24), k4, work in pat as est to end. 180 (200, 220, 236, 260, 282, 302) sts.

Row 7: Work in pat as est to 2nd marker, SM, ssp 1 (1, 0, 1, 0, 1, 1), p 7 (9, 13, 13, 16, 18, 20), k2, p 40 (44, 48, 50, 54, 58, 62), k2, p 44 (52, 60, 68, 74, 80, 88), k2, p 40 (44, 48, 50, 54, 58, 62), k2, p7 (9, 13, 13, 16, 18, 20), p2tog 1 (1, 0, 1, 0, 1, 1), work in pat as est to end. 178 (198, 220, 234, 260, 280, 300) sts.

Row 8: Work in pat as est to first marker, SM, k4, k2tog 0 (0, 0, 1, 0, 0), k 10 (12, 15, 16, 16, 21, 23), k2tog, k 36 (40, 44, 46, 50, 54, 58), ssk, k2, k2tog, k 40 (48, 56, 64, 70, 76, 84), ssk, k2, k2tog, k 36 (40, 44, 46, 50, 54, 58), ssk, k 10 (12, 15, 16, 16, 21, 23), ssk 0 (0, 0, 1, 0, 0), k4, work in pat as est to end. 172 (192, 214, 228, 252, 274, 294) sts.

Row 9: Work in pat as est to 2nd marker, SM, ssp 0 (0, 1, 0, 0, 0,

0), p 8 (10, 11, 14, 15, 19, 21), k2, p 38 (42, 46, 48, 52, 56, 60), k2, p 42 (50, 58, 66, 72, 78, 86), k2, p 38 (42, 46, 48, 52, 56, 60), k2, p 8 (10, 11, 14, 15, 19, 21), p2tog 0 (0, 1, 0, 0, 0, 0), work in pat as est to end. 172 (192, 212, 228, 252, 274, 294) sts.

Row 10: Work in pat as est to first marker, SM, k4, k2tog 0 (0, 0, 0, 0, 1, 1), k 10 (12, 14, 16, 17, 19, 21), k2tog, k 34 (38, 42, 44, 48, 52, 56), ssk, k2, k2tog 0 (0, 0, 0, 0, 1, 1), k 42 (50, 58, 66, 68, 74, 82), ssk 0 (0, 0, 0, 0, 1, 1), k2, k2tog, k 34 (38, 42, 44, 48, 52, 56), ssk, k 10 (12, 14, 16, 17, 19, 21), ssk 0 (0, 0, 0, 0, 1, 1), k4 work in pat as est to end. 168 (188, 208, 224, 246, 266, 286) sts.

Row 11: Work in pat as est to 2nd marker, SM, p 8 (10, 12, 14, 15, 18, 20), k2, p 36 (40, 44, 46, 50, 54, 58), k2, p 42 (50, 58, 66, 70, 76, 84), k2, p 36 (40, 44, 46, 50, 54, 58), k2, p 8 (10, 12, 14, 15, 18, 20), work in pat as est to end.

Row 12: Work in pat as est to first marker, SM, k4, k2tog 0 (0, 0, 1, 1, 0, 0), k 10 (12, 14, 14, 15, 20, 22), k2tog, k 32 (36, 40, 42, 46, 50, 54), ssk, k2, k2tog, k 38 (46, 54, 62, 66, 72, 80), ssk, k2, k2tog, k 32 (36, 40, 42, 46, 50, 54), ssk, k 10 (12, 14, 14, 15, 20, 22), ssk 0 (0, 0, 1, 1, 0, 0), k4, work in pat as est to end. 162 (182, 202, 216, 238, 260, 280) sts.

Row 13: Work in pat as est to 2nd marker, SM, ssp 0 (0, 0, 0, 0, 1, 1), p 8 (10, 12, 13, 14, 16, 18), k2, p 34 (38, 42, 44, 48, 52, 56), k2, p 40 (48, 56, 64, 68, 74, 82), k2, p 34 (38, 42, 44, 48, 52, 56), k2, p 8 (10, 12, 13, 14, 16, 18), p2tog 0 (0, 0, 0, 0, 1, 1), work in pat as est to end. 162 (182, 202, 216, 238, 258, 278) sts.

Row 14: Work in pat as est to first marker, SM, k4, k2tog 0 (1, 1, 0, 0, 0, 0), k 10 (10, 12, 15, 16, 19, 21), k2tog, k 30 (34, 38, 40, 44, 48, 52), ssk, k2, k2tog 0 (0, 0, 1, 1, 1, 1), k 40 (48, 56, 60, 64, 70, 78), ssk 0 (0, 0, 1, 1, 1, 1), k2, k2tog, k 30 (34, 38, 40, 44, 48, 52), ssk, k 10 (10, 12, 15, 16, 19, 21), ssk 0 (1, 1, 0, 0, 0, 0), k4, work in pat as est to end. 158 (176, 196, 210, 232, 252, 272) sts.

Row 15: Work in pat as est to 2nd marker, SM, p 8 (9, 11, 13, 14, 17, 19), k2, p 32 (36, 40, 42, 46, 50, 54), k2, p 40 (48, 56, 62, 66, 72, 80), k2, p 32 (36, 40, 42, 46, 50, 54), k2, p 8 (9, 11, 13, 14, 17, 19), work in pat as est to end.

Row 16: Work in pat as est to first marker, SM, k4, k2tog 0 (0, 0, 1, 1, 1, 1), k 10 (11, 13, 15, 14, 17, 19), k2tog, k 28 (32, 36, 38, 42, 46, 50), ssk, k2, k2tog, k 36 (44, 52, 58, 62, 68, 76), ssk, k2, k2tog, k 28 (32, 36, 38, 42, 46, 50), ssk, k 10 (11, 13, 15, 14, 17, 19), ssk 0 (0, 0, 1, 1, 1, 1), k4, work in pat as est to end. 152 (170, 190, 204, 224, 244, 264) sts.

Row 17: Work in pat as est to 2nd marker, SM, ssp 0 (0, 0, 1, 0, 0, 0), p 8 (9, 11, 11, 13, 16, 18), k2, p 30 (34, 38, 40, 44, 48, 52), k2, p 38 (46, 54, 60, 64, 70, 78), k2, p 30 (34, 38, 40, 44, 48, 52), k2, p 8 (9, 11, 11, 13, 16, 18), p2tog 0 (0, 0, 1, 0, 0, 0), work in pat as est to end. 152 (170, 190, 202, 224, 244, 264) sts.

Row 18: Work in pat as est to first marker, SM, k4, k2tog 1 (0, 0, 0, 0, 0, 0), k 8 (11, 13, 14, 15, 18, 20), k2tog, k 26 (30, 34, 36, 40, 44, 48), ssk, k2, k2tog 0 (0, 0, 1, 1, 1, 1), k 38 (46, 54, 56, 60, 66, 74), ssk 0 (0, 0, 1, 1, 1, 1), k2, k2tog, k 26 (30, 34, 36, 40, 44, 48), ssk, k 8 (11, 13, 14, 15, 18, 20), ssk 1 (0, 0, 0, 0, 0, 0), k4, work in pat as est to end. 146 (166, 186, 196, 218, 238, 258) sts.

Row 19: Work in pat as est to 2nd marker, SM, ssp 0 (0, 1, 0, 0, 1, 1), p 7 (9, 9, 12, 13, 14, 16), k2, p 28 (32, 36, 38, 42, 46, 50), k2, p 38 (46, 54, 58, 62, 68, 76), k2, p 28 (32, 36, 38, 42, 46, 50), k2, p 7 (9, 9, 12, 13, 14, 16), p2tog 0 (0, 1, 0, 0, 1, 1), work in pat as est to end. 146 (166, 184, 196, 218, 236, 256) sts.

Row 20: Work in pat as est to first marker, SM, k4, k2tog 0 (0, 0, 1, 0, 0), k 9 (11, 12, 14, 13, 17, 19), k2tog, k 24 (28, 32, 34, 38, 42, 46), ssk, k2, k2tog, k 34 (42, 50, 54, 58, 64, 72), ssk, k2, k2tog, k 24 (28, 32, 34, 38, 42, 46), ssk, k 9 (11, 12, 14, 13, 17, 19), ssk 0 (0, 0, 0, 1, 0, 0), k4, work in pat as est to end. 140 (160, 178, 190, 210, 230, 250) sts.

Row 21: Work in pat as est to 2nd marker, SM, ssp 0 (1, 0, 0, 0, 0, 0), p 7 (7, 10, 12, 12, 15, 17), k2, p 26 (30, 34, 36, 40, 44, 48), k2, p 36 (44, 52, 56, 60, 66, 74), k2, p 26 (30, 34, 36, 40, 44, 48), k2, p 7 (7, 10, 12, 12, 15, 17), p2tog 0 (1, 0, 0, 0, 0, 0), work in pat as est to end. 140 (158, 178, 190, 210, 230, 250) sts.

Row 22: Work in pat as est to first marker, SM, k4, k2tog 0 (0, 1, 0, 1, 1), k 9 (10, 12, 12, 14, 15, 17), k2tog, k 22 (26, 30, 32, 36, 40, 44), ssk, k2, k2tog 0 (0, 0, 1, 1, 1, 1), k 36 (44, 52, 52, 56, 62, 70), ssk 0 (0, 0, 1, 1, 1, 1), k2, k2tog, k 22 (26, 30, 32, 36, 40, 44), ssk, k 9 (10, 12, 12, 14, 15, 17), ssk 0 (0, 0, 1, 0, 1, 1), k4, work in pat as est to end. 136 (154, 174, 182, 204, 222, 242) sts.

Row 23: Work in pat as est to 2nd marker, SM, p 7 (8, 10, 11, 12, 14, 16), k2, p 24 (28, 32, 34, 38, 42, 46), k2, p 36 (44, 52, 54, 58, 64, 72), k2, p 24 (28, 32, 34, 38, 42, 46), k2, p 7 (8, 10, 11, 12, 14, 16), work in pat as est to end.

Row 24: Work in pat as est to first marker, SM, k4, k2tog 0 (0, 1, 0, 1, 0, 0), k 9 (10, 10, 13, 12, 16, 18), k2tog, k 20 (24, 28, 30, 34, 38, 42), ssk, k2, k2tog, k 32 (40, 48, 50, 54, 60, 68), ssk, k2, k2tog, k 20 (24, 28, 30, 34, 38, 42), ssk, k 9 (10, 10, 13, 12, 16, 18), ssk 0 (0, 1, 0, 1, 0, 0), k4, work in pat as est to end. 130 (148, 166, 176, 196, 216, 236) sts.

Row 25: Work in pat as est to 2nd marker, SM, ssp 0 (0, 0, 0, 0, 1, 1), p 7 (8, 9, 11, 11, 12, 14), k2, p 22 (26, 30, 32, 36, 40, 44), k2, p 34 (42, 50, 52, 56, 62, 70), k2, p 22 (26, 30, 32, 36, 40, 44), k2, p 7 (8, 9, 11, 11, 12, 14), p2tog 0 (0, 0, 0, 0, 1, 1), work in pat as est to end. 130 (148, 166, 176, 196, 214, 234) sts.

Row 26: Work in pat as est to first marker, SM, k4, k2tog 0 (0, 1, 0, 0, 0), k 9 (10, 11, 11, 13, 15, 17), k2tog, k 18 (22, 26, 28, 32, 36, 40), ssk, k2, k2tog 0 (0, 1, 1, 1, 1, 1), k 34 (42, 46, 48, 52, 58, 66), ssk 0 (0, 1, 1, 1, 1, 1), k2, k2tog, k 18 (22, 26, 28, 32, 36, 40), ssk, k 9 (10, 11, 11, 13, 15, 17), ssk 0 (0, 0, 1, 0, 0, 0), k4, work in pat as est to end. 126 (144, 160, 168, 190, 208, 228) sts.

Row 27: Work in pat as est to 2nd marker, SM, p 7 (8, 9, 10, 11, 13, 15), k2, p 20 (24, 28, 30, 34, 38, 42), k2, p 34 (42, 48, 50, 54, 60, 68), k2, p 20 (24, 28, 30, 34, 38, 42), k2, p 7 (8, 9, 10, 11, 13, 15), work in pat as est to end.

Row 28: Work in pat as est to first marker, SM, k4, k2tog 0 (1, 0, 0, 1, 1, 1), k 9 (8, 11, 12, 11, 13, 15), k2tog, k 16 (20, 24, 26, 30, 34, 38), ssk, k2, k2tog, k 30 (38, 44, 46, 50, 56, 64), ssk, k2, k2tog, k 16 (20, 24, 26, 30, 34, 38), ssk, k 9 (8, 11, 12, 11, 13, 15), ssk 0 (1, 0, 0, 1, 1, 1), k4, work in pat as est to end. 120 (136, 154, 162, 182, 200, 220) sts.

Row 29: Work in pat as est to 2nd marker, SM, ssp 1 (0, 1, 0, 0, 0, 0), p 5 (7, 7, 10, 10, 12, 14), k2, p 18 (22, 26, 28, 32, 36, 40), k2, p 32 (40, 46, 48, 52, 58, 66), k2, p 18 (22, 26, 28, 32, 36, 40), k2, p 5 (7, 7, 10, 10, 12, 14), p2tog 0 (1, 0, 0, 0, 0), work in pat as est to end. 118 (136, 152, 162, 182, 200, 220) sts.

Row 30: Work in pat as est to first marker, SM, k4, k2tog 0 (0, 1, 0, 0, 0), k 8 (9, 10, 10, 12, 14, 16), k2tog, k 14 (18, 22, 24, 28, 32, 36), ssk, k2, k2tog 0 (0, 1, 1, 1, 1, 1), k 32 (40, 42, 44, 48, 54, 62), ssk 0 (0, 1, 1, 1, 1, 1), k2, k2tog, k 14 (18, 22, 24, 28, 32, 36), ssk, k 8 (9, 10,

10, 12, 14, 16), ssk 0 (0, 0, 1, 0, 0, 0), k4, work in pat as est to end. 114 (132, 146, 154, 176, 194, 214) sts.

Row 31: Work in pat as est to 2nd marker, SM, ssp 0 (0, 0, 0, 0, 1, 1), p 6 (7, 8, 9, 10, 10, 12), k2, p 16 (20, 24, 26, 30, 34, 38), k2, p 32 (40, 44, 46, 50, 56, 64), k2, p 16 (20, 24, 26, 30, 34, 38), k2, p 6 (7, 8, 9, 10, 10, 12), p2tog 0 (0, 0, 0, 0, 1, 1), work in pat as est to end. 114 (132, 146, 154, 176, 192, 212) sts.

Row 32: Work in pat as est to first marker, SM, k4, k2tog 1 (0, 0, 0, 1, 0, 0), k 6 (9, 10, 11, 10, 13, 15), k2tog, k 12 (16, 20, 22, 26, 30, 34), ssk, k2, k2tog, k 28 (36, 40, 42, 46, 52, 60), ssk, k2, k2tog, k 12 (16, 20, 22, 26, 30, 34) ssk, k 6 (9, 10, 11, 10, 13, 15), ssk 1 (0, 0, 0, 1, 0, 0), k4, work in pat as est to end. 106 (126, 140, 148, 168, 186, 206) sts.

Row 33: Work in pat as est to 2nd marker, SM, p 5 (7, 8, 9, 9, 11, 13), k2, p 14 (18, 22, 24, 28, 32, 36), k2, p 30 (38, 42, 44, 48, 54, 62), k2, p 14 (18, 22, 24, 28, 32, 36), k2, p 5 (7, 8, 9, 9, 11, 13), work in pat as est to end.

Row 34: Work in pat as est to first marker, SM, k4, k2tog 1 (0, 1, 1, 0, 1, 1), k 5 (9, 8, 9, 11, 11, 13), k2tog, k 10 (14, 18, 20, 24, 28, 32), ssk, k2, k2tog 0 (1, 1, 1, 1, 1, 1), k 30 (34, 38, 40, 44, 50, 58), ssk 0 (1, 1, 1, 1, 1, 1), k2, k2tog, k 10 (14, 18, 20, 24, 28, 32), ssk, k 5 (9, 8, 9, 11, 11, 13), ssk 1 (0, 1, 1, 0, 1, 1), k4, work in pat as est to end. 100 (120, 132, 140, 162, 178, 198) sts.

Row 35: Work in pat as est to 2nd marker, SM, ssp 0 (1, 0, 0, 0, 0, 0), p 4 (5, 7, 8, 9, 10, 12), k2, p 12 (16, 20, 22, 26, 30, 34), k2, p 30 (36, 40, 42, 46, 52, 60), k2, p 12 (16, 20, 22, 26, 30, 34), k2, p 4 (5, 7, 8, 9, 10, 12), p2tog 0 (1, 0, 0, 0, 0, 0), work in pat as est to end. 100 (118, 132, 140, 162, 178, 198) sts.

Row 36: Work in pat as est to first marker, SM, k4, k2tog 0 (0, 0, 1, 0, 0), k 6 (8, 9, 10, 9, 12, 14), k2tog, k 8 (12, 16, 18, 22, 26, 30), ssk, k2, k2tog, k 26 (32, 36, 38, 42, 48, 56), ssk, k2, k2tog, k 8 (12, 16, 18, 22, 26, 30), ssk, k 6 (8, 9, 10, 9, 12, 14), ssk 0 (0, 0, 0, 1, 0, 0), k4, work in pat as est to end. 94 (112, 126, 134, 154, 172, 192) sts.

Row 37: Work in pat as est to 2nd marker, SM, ssp 1 (1, 0, 0, 0, 1, 1), p 2 (4, 7, 8, 8, 8, 10), k2, p 10 (14, 18, 20, 24, 28, 32), k2, p 28 (34, 38, 40, 44, 50, 58), k2, p 10 (14, 18, 20, 24, 28, 32), k2, p 2 (4, 7, 8, 8, 8, 10), p2tog 1 (1, 0, 0, 0, 1, 1), work in pat as est to end. 92 (110, 126, 134, 154, 170, 190) sts.

Row 38: Work in pat as est to first marker, SM, k4, k2tog 1 (0, 1, 1, 0, 0, 0), k 3 (7, 7, 8, 10, 11, 13), k2tog, k 6 (10, 14, 16, 20, 24, 28), ssk, k2, k2tog, k 24 (30, 34, 36, 40, 46, 54), ssk, k2, k2tog, k 6 (10, 14, 16, 20, 24, 28), ssk, k 3 (7, 7, 8, 10, 11, 13), ssk 1 (0, 1, 1, 0, 0, 0), k4, work in pat as est to end. 84 (104, 118, 126, 148, 164, 184) sts.

Row 39: Work in pat as est to 2nd marker, SM, ssp 0 (1, 1, 1, 0, 0, 0), p 2 (3, 4, 5, 8, 9, 11), k2, ssp, p 4 (8, 12, 14, 18, 22, 26), p2tog, k2, ssp 0 (1, 1, 1, 1, 1, 1), p 26 (28, 32, 34, 38, 44, 52), p2tog 0 (1, 1, 1, 1, 1, 1), k2, ssp, p 4 (3, 12, 14, 18, 22, 26), p2tog, k2, p 2 (6, 4, 5, 8, 9, 11), p2tog 0 (1, 1, 1, 0, 0, 0), work in pat as est to end. 80 (96, 110, 118, 142, 158, 178) sts.

Row 40: Work in pat as est to first marker, SM, k4, k2tog, k 2 (4, 5, 6, 8, 9, 11), k2tog, k 2 (6, 10, 12, 16, 20, 24), ssk, k2, k2tog, k 22 (26, 30, 32, 36, 42, 50), ssk, k2, k2tog, k 2 (6, 10, 12, 16, 20, 24), ssk, k 6 (4, 5, 6, 8, 9, 11), ssk, k4, work in pat as est to end. 72 (88, 102, 110, 134, 150, 170) sts.

Row 41: Work in pat as est to 2nd marker, SM, p 1 (3, 4, 5, 7, 8, 10), k2, ssp, p 0 (4, 8, 10, 14, 18, 22), p2tog, k2, ssp, p 20 (24, 28,

30, 34, 40, 48), p2tog, k2, ssp, p 0 (4, 8, 10, 14, 18, 22), p2tog, k2, p 1 (3, 4, 5, 7, 8, 10), work in pat as est to end. 66 (82, 96, 104, 128, 144, 164) sts.

Sizes – (24, 28, 32, 36, 40, 44)" only:

Row 42: Work in pat as est to first marker, SM, k4, k2tog 0 (1, 1, 1, 0, 0, 0), k 0 (3, 4, 5, 9, 10, 12), k2tog, k 0 (2, 6, 8, 12, 16, 20), ssk, k2, k2tog, k 0 (22, 26, 28, 32, 38, 46), ssk, k2, k2tog, k 0 (2, 6, 8, 12, 16, 20), ssk, k 0 (3, 4, 5, 9, 10, 12), ssk 0 (1, 1, 1, 0, 0, 0), k4, work in pat as est to end. – (74, 88, 96, 122, 138, 158) sts.

Row 43: Work in pat as est to 2nd marker, SM, ssp 0 (1, 1, 1, 0, 1, 1), p 0 (0, 1, 2, 7, 6, 8), k2, ssp, p 0 (0, 4, 6, 10, 14, 18), p2tog, k2, ssp, p 0 (20, 24, 26, 30, 36, 44), p2tog, k2, ssp, p 0 (0, 4, 6, 10, 14, 18), p2tog, k2, p 0 (0, 1, 2, 7, 6, 8), p2tog 0 (1, 1, 1, 0, 1, 1), work in pat as est to end. – (66, 80, 88, 116, 130, 150) sts.

Sizes – (–, 28, 32, 36, 40, 44)" only:

Row 44: Work in pat as est to first marker, SM, k4, k2tog 0 (0, 1, 1, 1, 0, 0), k 0 (0, 2, 3, 7, 9, 11), k2tog, k 0 (0, 2, 4, 8, 12, 16), ssk, k2, k2tog, k 0 (0, 22, 24, 28, 34, 42), ssk, k2, k2tog, k 0 (0, 2, 4, 8, 12, 16), ssk, k 0 (0, 2, 3, 7, 9, 11), ssk 0 (0, 1, 1, 1, 0, 0), k4, work in pat as est to end. – (–, 72, 80, 108, 124, 144) sts.

Row 45: Work in pat as est to 2nd marker, SM, p 0 (0, 1, 2, 6, 7, 9), k2, ssp, p 0 (0, 0, 2, 6, 10, 14), p2tog, k2, ssp, p 0 (0, 20, 22, 26, 32, 40), p2tog, k2, ssp, p 0 (0, 0, 2, 6, 10, 14), p2tog, k2, p 0 (0, 1, 2, 6, 7, 9), work in pat as est to end. – (–, 66, 74, 102, 118, 138) sts.

Sizes – (–, –, 32, 36, 40, 44)" only:

Row 46: Work in pat as est to first marker, SM, k4, k2tog, k 0 (0, 0, 2, 6, 7, 9), k2tog, k 0 (0, 0, 0, 4, 8, 12), ssk, k2, k2tog, k 0 (0, 0, 20, 24, 30, 38), ssk, k2, k2tog, k 0 (0, 0, 0, 4, 8, 12), ssk, k 0 (0, 0, 2, 6, 7, 9), ssk, k4, work in pat as est to end. – (–, –, 66, 94, 110, 130) sts.

Sizes – (–, –, –, 36, 40, 44)" only:

Row 47: Work in pat as est to 2nd marker, ssp 0 (0, 0, 0, 1, 1, 0), p 0 (0, 0, 0, 3, 4, 8), k2, ssp, p 0 (0, 0, 0, 2, 6, 10), p2tog, k2, ssp, p 0 (0, 0, 0, 22, 28, 36), p2tog, k2, ssp, p 0 (0, 0, 0, 2, 6, 10), p2tog, k2, p 0 (0, 0, 0, 3, 4, 8), p2tog 0 (0, 0, 0, 1, 1, 0), work in pat as est to end. – (–, –, –, 86, 102, 124) sts.

Row 48: Work in pat as est to first marker, k4, k2tog, k 0 (0, 0, 0, 4, 5, 8), k2tog, k 0 (0, 0, 0, 0, 4, 8), ssk, k2, k2tog, k 0 (0, 0, 0, 20, 26, 34), ssk, k2, k2tog, k 0 (0, 0, 0, 0, 4, 8), ssk, k 0 (0, 0, 0, 4, 5, 8), ssk, k4, work in pat as est to end. – (–, –, –, 78, 94, 116) sts.

Sizes – (–, –, –, –, 40, 44)" only:

Row 49: Work in pat as est to 2nd marker, ssp, p 0 (0, 0, 0, 0, 2, 5), k2, ssp, p 0 (0, 0, 0, 0, 2, 6), p2tog, k2, sssp, p 0 (0, 0, 0, 0, 22, 30), p3tog, k2, ssp, p 0 (0, 0, 0, 0, 2, 6), p2tog, k2, p 0 (0, 0, 0, 0, 2, 5), p2tog, work in pat as est to end. – (–, –, –, –, 84, 106) sts.

Sizes – (–,–,–,–,–, 44)" only:

Row 50: Work in pat as est to first marker, k4, k2tog, k 0 (0, 0, 0, 0, 0, 6), k2tog, k 0 (0, 0, 0, 0, 0, 4), ssk, k2, k3tog, k 0 (0, 0, 0, 0, 0, 26), sssk, k2, k2tog, k 0 (0, 0, 0, 0, 0, 4), ssk, k 0 (0, 0, 0, 0, 0, 6), ssk, k4, work in pat as est to end. – (–, –, –, –, –, 96) sts.

Row 51: Work in pat as est to 2nd marker, ssp, p 0 (0, 0, 0, 0, 0, 3), k2, ssp, p 0 (0, 0, 0, 0, 0, 2), p2tog, k2, sssp, p 0 (0, 0, 0, 0, 0, 22), p3tog, k2, ssp, p 0 (0, 0, 0, 0, 0, 2), p2tog, k2, p 0 (0, 0, 0, 0, 0, 3), p2tog, work in pat as est to end. – (–, –, –, –, –, 86) sts.

Collar

The border is knit around the last stitches from the top of the yoke. On every second row, you will k2tog one of the collar stitches to the border as it moves around. Knit from where you ended the yoke to the center back, then knit the other side to meet it.

Side one:
Row 1: Sl1, k 3 (3, 3, 3, 4, 4, 4), p1, [k2, p1] 2 (2, 2, 2, 3, 3, 3) times, k3, k2tog, turn.
Row 2: K2, [p2, k1] 3 (3, 3, 3, 4, 4, 4) times, p2, k1 (1, 1, 1, 2, 2, 2), p1.

Side two:
Row 1: K4, [p1, k2] 2 (2, 2, 2, 3, 3, 3) times, p1, k 4 (4, 4, 4, 5, 5, 5).
Row 2: Sl1 wyif, k 1 (1, 1, 1, 2, 2, 2), [p2, k1] 3 (3, 3, 3, 4, 4, 4) times, p2, k1, k2tog, turn.

Graft or three needle bind off the last stitches, closing up the back of the collar.

Belt

Block the cardigan to size. With WS facing, and starting at the bottom, pick up 13 stitches through the slipped stitches on the opposite side as the slit for the belt to pass through. Begin working belt, following written instructions or charts. Odd-numbered rows are WS and must be read left to right on the charts. When you are close to being done with the belt, try the cardigan on and see if you can pin it closed. You may want to make the belt slightly longer or shorter, and this is why you should block the cardigan first. An Alternate Ending is also provided, should you wish to add length without working an entire cable pattern repeat.

Row 1: Sl1 wyif, k3, p1, [k1, p1] 2 times, k3, p1.
Row 2: Sl1, k1, RKI, p1, LKI, p1, k1, RKI, p1, k1, p1, LKI, k1, p1, RKI, p1, LKI, k2.
Row 3: Sl1 wyif, [k1, p1] 2 times, k1, p2, k1, p1, k1, p2, k1, [p1, k1] 2 times, p1.
Row 4: Sl1, [k2, p1, k1, p1] 3 times, k3.
Row 5: Rep Row 3.
Row 6: Sl1, k1, 5/5 LC, [k1, p1] 2 times, k3.
Rows 7-11: Rep Rows 3-4 2 times, then work Row 3 once more.
Row 12: Sl1, k2, [p1, k1] 2 times, 5/5 RC, k2.
Row 13: Sl1 wyif, [k1, p1] 2 times, [k1, p2, k1, p1] 2 times, [k1, p1] 2 times.
Row 14: Sl1, [k2, p1, k1, p1] 3 times, k3.
Rows 15-17: Rep Rows 13-14, then work Row 13 once more.
Row 18: Sl1, k1, 5/5 LC, [k1, p1] 2 times, k3.
Rows 19-23: Rep Rows 13-14 2 times, then work Row 13 once more.

Work Rows 12-23 a total of 6 (8, 10, 12, 14, 16, 18) times, or to achieve desired length.

Row 24: Sl1, k2, [p1, k1] 2 times, 5/5 RC, k2.
Row 25: Sl1 wyif, [k1, p1] 2 times, [k1, p2, k1, p1] 2 times, [k1, p1] 2 times.

Button hole:
First Side:
Row 26: Sl1, k2, [p1, k1] 2 times.

Row 27: Sl1 wyif, [k1, p1] 2 times, k2.
Row 28: Sl1, k2, [p1, k1] 2 times.
Row 29: Sl1 wyif, [k1, p1] 2 times, k2.

Rep Rows 28-29 a total of 3 times for a 2 inch diameter button as suggested, or 2 times for a 1.5 inch button, or not at all for a 1 inch button.

Row 30: Sl1, k2, [p1, k1] 2 times.
Row 31: Sl1 wyif, [k1, p1] 2 times, k2.

Other side:
Row 26: K1, p1, k1, p1, sssk, k4tog, k1.
Row 27: K2, [p1, k1] 2 times, p1.
Row 28: [K1, p1] twice, k3.
Row 29: K2, [p1, k1] 2 times, p1.

Rep Rows 28-29 the same number of times as you did on the first side.

Row 30: [K1, p1] 2 times, k3.
Row 31: K2, [p1, k1] 2 times, p1.

Join buttonhole sides:
Row 32: Sl1, k2, p1, k1, p1, k2tog, [p1, k1] 2 times, k2.
Row 33: Sl1 wyif, [k1, p1] 6 times.
Row 34: Sl1, k3, s3tog-k2tog-p3sso, k4.
Row 35: Sl1 wyif, [k1, p1] 4 times.
Row 36: Sl1, k1, s3tog-k2tog-p3sso, k2.
Row 37: K1, p3tog, k1.

BO all sts.

Alternate ending:

If you want to end your belt between an even number of repeats of rows 12-23, you may work this alternate ending to gain an extra inch in length.

Row 24a: Sl1, k2, [p1, k1] 2 times, 5/5 RC, k2.
Row 25a: Sl1 wyif, [k1, p1] 2 times, [k1, p2, k1, p1] 2 times, [k1, p1] 2 times.
Row 26a: Sl1, [k2, p1, k1, p1] 3 times, k3.
Row 27a: Sl1 wyif, [k1, p1] 2 times, [k1, p2, k1, p1] 2 times, [k1, p1] 2 times.
Rows 28a-29a: Rep Rows 26a-27a.
Row 30a: Sl1, k1, 5/5 LC, [k1, p1] 2 times, k3.
Row 31a: Sl1 wyif, [k1, p1] 2 times, [k1, p2, k1, p1] 2 times, [k1, p1] 2 times.

Button hole:
First side:
Row 32a: Sl1, s4k, k3tog, [p1, k1] 2 times.
Row 33a: Sl1 wyif, [k1, p1] 2 times, k2.
Row 34a: Sl1, k2, [p1, k1] 2 times.
Row 35a: Sl1 wyif, [k1, p1] 2 times, k2 .

Repeat Rows 34a-35a a total of 3 times for a 2 inch diameter button as suggested, or 2 times for a 1.5 inch button, or not at all for a 1 inch button.

Row 36a: Sl1, k2, [p1, k1] 2 times.
Row 37a: Sl1 wyif, [k1, p1] 2 times, k2.

Cabled Belt Chart

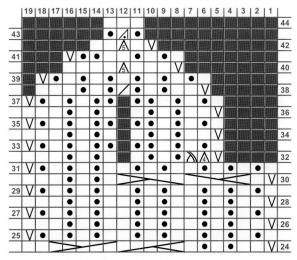

Alternate Ending

Legend:

knit
RS: knit stitch
WS: purl stitch

purl
RS: purl stitch
WS: knit stitch

No Stitch
Placeholder - No stitch made.

slip
RS: Slip stitch as if to purl, holding yarn in back
WS: Slip stitch as if to purl, holding yarn in front

make one right
RS: Place a firm backward loop over the right needle, so that the yarn end goes towards the back

make one left
RS: Place a firm backward loop over the right needle, so that the yarn end goes towards the front

sssk
RS: (Slip 1 as if to knit) 3 times; insert left-hand needle from the front to the back of all stitches at the same time and knit them together.

k4tog
RS: Knit four stitches together as one

k2tog
Knit two stitches together as one

k5tog
Knit five stitches together as one

p3tog
Purl three stitches together as one

5/5 LC

5/5 RC

Other side:

Row 32a: [k1, p1] 2 times, k3.

Row 33a: k2, [p1, k1] 2 times, p1.

Row 34a: [k1, p1] 2 times, k3.

Row 35a: k2, [p1, k1] 2 times, p1.

Repeat 34a-35a the same number of times as you did on the first side.

Row 36a: [k1, p1] 2 times, k3.

Row 37a: k2, [p1, k1] 2 times, p1.

Join buttonhole sides:

Row 38a: Sl1, k2, p1, k1, p1, k2tog, p1, k1, p1, k3.

Row 39a: Sl1 wyif, [k1, p1] 6 times.

Row 40a: Sl1, k3, s3tog-k2tog-p3sso, k4.

Row 41a: Sl1 wyif, [k1, p1] 4 times.

Row 42a: Sl1, k1, s3tog-k2tog-p3sso, k2.

Row 43a: K1, p3tog, k1.

BO all sts.

Finishing

Weave in ends, wash and block to diagram. Sew a patch of heavy duty stabilizer below where the button belongs, an oval about 2x3 inches works well. Stitch it down to the backs of the purls or knits, and then sew the button onto it.

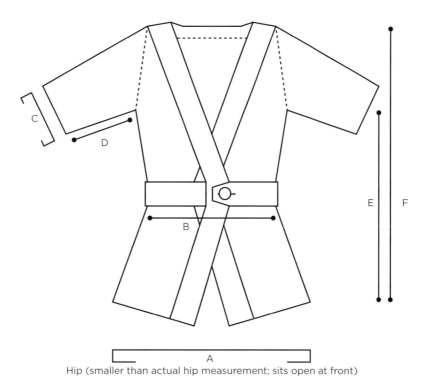

Hip (smaller than actual hip measurement; sits open at front)

A 26 (30, 33, 37, 43, 47, 50)"
B 20 (24, 28, 32, 36, 40, 44)"
C 12 (13, 14, 15, 16, 17, 19)"
D 10"
E 16"
F 22 (22, 22, 23, 23, 23, 23)"

BELLFLOWER

by Jill Wright

FINISHED MEASUREMENTS

34 (38, 42, 46, 50, 54, 58, 62, 66)"
finished bust measurement; garment is
meant to be worn with 2-4" of positive
ease
30½ (31, 31½, 31½, 32, 32½, 32½, 33, 33½)"
length, not including neck band
Sample is size 38" bust

YARN

Knit Picks Swish Bulky (100% Superwash
Merino Wool; 137 yards/100g):
Doe 26073, 9 (10, 11, 12, 13, 14, 15, 16, 17)
balls

NEEDLES

US 10 (6mm) 32" or longer circular
needles, or size to obtain gauge

NOTIONS

Yarn needle
Stitch markers
Stitch holders
Cable needle
4 buttons, approx. 2" in diameter

GAUGE

15 sts and 21 rows = 4" in 5x2 Rib,
blocked.

Bellflower

Notes:

This A-line jacket is worked from the bottom up in one piece to armholes, and is then split into fronts and back. Sleeves are worked back and forth, then sewn in place.

Special Stitches

C6F: cable 6 front – sl 3 sts onto cable needle and hold in front, k3 from left hand needle, k3 from cable needle.

C6B: cable 6 back – sl 3 sts onto cable needle and hold in back, k3 from left hand needle, k3 from cable needle.

Stockinette Stitch

Row 1: K.

Row 2: P.

5x2 Rib (worked over a multiple of 7 sts plus 2)

Row 1: K2, *k5, k2; rep from * to end.

Row 2: P2, *k5, p2; rep from * to end.

Rep rows 1 and 2 for 5x2 rib.

Braided Cable (worked over 9 sts)

Row 1 (RS): K.

Rows 2, 4, 6, and 8: P.

Row 3: C6F, k3.

Row 5: K.

Row 7: K3, C6B.

Rep rows 1-8 for Braided Cable.

1-Row Buttonhole

Sl 1 st to right needle, * sl 1 more st to right needle, pass 1st st over 2nd st; rep from * twice more, sl last st back on left needle, CO 3 sts using backwards loop method.

Backwards Loop CO

Holding your needle in your right hand, grasp the working yarn in your left hand.

Pass the working yarn around your left thumb from back to front. Slip the needle tip under the loop around your thumb. Pull your thumb out of the loop and tug on the working yarn to tighten up the stitch.

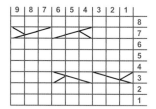

Legend:

 knit
knit stitch

c3 over 3 left
sl3 to CN, hold in front. k3, k3 from CN

c3 over 3 right
sl3 to CN, hold in back. k3, then k3 from CN

DIRECTIONS

Pockets (make 2)

CO 22 sts and work in Stockinette st for 8". Place all sts on a holder. Cut yarn, leaving a 1-yard tail for sewing pocket to jacket later.

Jacket

CO 166 (182, 198, 214, 230, 242, 258, 274, 290) sts.

Setup row (RS): K3 (3, 3, 4, 4, 4, 5, 5, 5), p5, k2, p8, work 9 sts in Braided Cable, p8, work 9 (9, 16, 16, 23, 23, 30, 30, 37) sts in 5x2 Rib, p 0 (8, 2, 8, 2, 8, 0, 8, 2), work 9 (9, 16, 16, 23, 23, 30, 30, 37) sts in 5x2 Rib, p8, work 9 sts in Braided Cable, p8, k2, p 6 (6, 6, 8, 8, 8, 10, 10, 10), k2, p8, work 9 sts in Braided Cable, p8, work 9 (9, 16, 16, 23, 23, 30, 30, 37) sts in 5x2 Rib, p 0 (8, 2, 8, 2, 8, 0, 8, 2), work 9 (9, 16, 16, 23, 23, 30, 30, 37) sts in 5x2 Rib, p8, work 9 sts in Braided Cable, p8, k2, p5, k3 (3, 3, 4, 4, 4, 5, 5, 5).

Work in established pat until piece measures 8", ending after a WS row. Work any sts that are not part of the pat panels as they appear – knitting the knits and purling the purls.

Dec Row (RS): *Work in pat to 2 sts before Braided Cable, p2tog, work 9 sts in established Braided Cable, p2tog; rep from * 3 more times, work in pat to end – 158 (174, 190, 206, 222, 234, 250, 266, 282) sts.

Work evenly in established pat until piece measures 10", ending after a WS row.

Place Pockets

Work 12 (12, 12, 13, 13, 13, 14, 14, 14) sts in established pat, place next 22 sts on a holder, work 22 sts from pocket in established jacket pat, work to last 34 (34, 34, 35, 35, 35, 36, 36, 36) sts, attach second pocket same as first, work to end.

Work evenly in established pats until piece measures 14", ending after a WS row.

Work Dec Row once – 150 (166, 182, 198, 214, 226, 242, 258, 274) sts.

Work evenly until piece measures 17 (16.75, 16.5, 15.75, 15.25, 15.25, 15, 14.75)", ending after a WS row.

Buttonhole Row (RS): Work 4 sts in established pat, work 1-Row Buttonhole, work in established pat to end.

Work evenly until piece measures 20", ending after a WS row.

Work Dec Row once – 142 (158, 174, 190, 206, 218, 234, 250, 266) sts.

Work evenly until piece measures 21 (21, 21, 20.5, 20.5, 20.5, 20.5, 20.5, 20.5)".

Work Buttonhole Row.

Work evenly until piece measures 22 (22, 22, 21.5, 21.5, 21.5, 21, 21, 21)", ending after a WS row.

Separate at Armholes

Next row (RS): Work 37 (40, 41, 42, 44, 44, 45, 47, 49) sts in established pat for Right Front, BO 2 (4, 10, 16, 20, 26, 32, 36, 40) sts, work 64 (70, 72, 74, 78, 78, 80, 84, 88) sts for Back, BO 2 (4, 10, 16, 20, 26, 32, 36, 40) sts, work to end for Left Front.

Left Front

Work evenly across Left Front sts only until piece measures 5.5 (6, 6.5, 7, 7.5, 8, 8.5, 9, 9.5)" from armhole, ending after a RS row.

Shape Neck

Next row (WS): Work 10 (10, 10, 11, 11, 11, 12, 12, 12) sts in established pat and place these sts on a holder, work to end.

Continuing to work in pat, dec 1 st at neck edge every row 9 times – 18 (21, 22, 22, 24, 24, 24, 26, 28) sts.

Work evenly until piece measures 7.5 (8, 8.5, 9, 9.5, 10, 10.5, 11, 11.5)" from armhole, ending after a WS row.

Shape Shoulder

BO 6 (7, 7, 7, 8, 8, 8, 8, 9) sts at beg of next RS row, then BO 6 (7, 7, 7, 8, 8, 8, 9, 9) sts at beg of next RS row, then BO rem 6 (7, 8, 8, 8, 8, 8, 9, 10) sts on next RS row..

Back

With WS facing, rejoin yarn to Back sts, and work evenly in established pat until piece measures 7.5 (8, 8.5, 9, 9.5, 10, 10.5, 11, 11.5)" from armhole.

Shape Shoulders

BO 6 (7, 7, 7, 8, 8, 8, 8, 8) sts at beg of next 2 rows, then 6 (7, 7, 7, 8, 8, 8, 9, 9) sts at beg of next 2 rows, then 6 (7, 8, 8, 8, 8, 8, 9, 10) sts at beg of next 2 rows.

Place rem 28 (28, 28, 30, 30, 30, 32, 32, 34) sts on a holder.

Right Front

With WS facing, rejoin yarn to Right Front sts, and work evenly in established pat until piece measures 4 (4.25, 4.5, 4.75, 5, 5.25, 5.25, 5.5, 5.75)" from last buttonhole, ending after a WS row, then work Buttonhole Row.

Work evenly until armhole measures 5.5 (6, 6.5, 7, 7.5, 8, 8.5, 9, 9.5)", ending after a WS row.

Shape Neck

Next row (RS): Work 10 (10, 10, 11, 11, 11, 12, 12, 12) sts in established pat and place these sts on a holder, work to end.

Continuing to work in pat, dec 1 st at neck edge every row 9 times – 18 (21, 22, 22, 24, 24, 24, 26, 28) sts.

Work evenly until piece measures 7.5 (8, 8.5, 9, 9.5, 10, 10.5, 11, 11.5)" from armhole, ending after a RS row.

Shape Shoulder

BO 6 (7, 7, 7, 8, 8, 8, 8, 9) sts at beg of next WS row, then 6 (7, 7, 7, 8, 8, 8, 9, 9) sts at beg of next RS row, then BO rem 6 (7, 8, 8, 8, 8, 8, 9, 10) sts.

Sleeves (make 2)

CO 59 (63, 67, 71, 75, 79, 83, 87, 89) sts.

Setup row (RS): K6 (1, 3, 5, 7, 2, 4, 6, 7), p5, work 9 (16, 16, 16, 16, 23, 23, 23, 23) sts in 5x2 Rib, p5, work 9 sts in Braided Cable, p5, work 9 (16, 16, 16, 16, 23, 23, 23, 23) sts in 5x2 Rib, p5, k6 (1, 3, 5, 7, 2, 4, 6, 7).

Work in established pat until piece measures 17 (17.25, 18, 19.25, 19.75, 20.5, 21.5, 22, 22.5)". Work any sts that are not part of the pat panels as they appear – knitting the knits and purling the purls.

BO all sts loosely in pat.

Finishing

Weave in loose ends. Block pieces to measurements.

Sew shoulder seams.

Neckband

With RS facing, rejoin yarn at Right Front neck edge.

Row 1 (RS): Work in established pat across 10 (10, 10, 11, 11, 11, 12, 12, 12) sts from holder, pu&k 10 sts up Right Front neck edge (5 sts from purl section, and 5 more from cabled section), work in established pat across 28 (28, 28, 30, 30, 30, 32, 32, 34) sts from back neck holder, pu&k 10 sts down Left Front neck edge (5 sts from cabled section, and 5 more from purl section),work in established pat across 10 (10, 10, 11, 11, 11, 12, 12, 12) sts from Left Front neck holder – 68 (68, 68, 72, 72, 72, 76, 76, 76) sts.
Row 2: P3 (3, 3, 4, 4, 4, 5, 5, 5), k5, p2, k5, p9, k5, p2, k6 (6, 6, 8, 8, 8, 10, 10, 10), p2, k5, p9, k5, p2, k5, p3 (3, 3, 4, 4, 4, 5, 5, 5).

Work in established pats, continuing Braided Cable up Neckband, until Neckband measures 1.5" from picked up edge, ending after a WS row.

Work Buttonhole Row.

Work evenly in established pat until Neckband measures 3" from picked up edge, then BO all sts loosely in pat.

Seaming

Sew sleeve seams, then sew sleeves in place. Sew down pockets on inside of jacket.

Pocket Tops

With RS facing, place held pocket sts back onto needle. Join yarn at right end of pocket opening, work in st pat as established for 1". BO in pat. Sew sides of pocket tops to body.

Rep for other pocket.

Sew buttons onto left front, corresponding to buttonholes.

Weave in remaining loose ends.

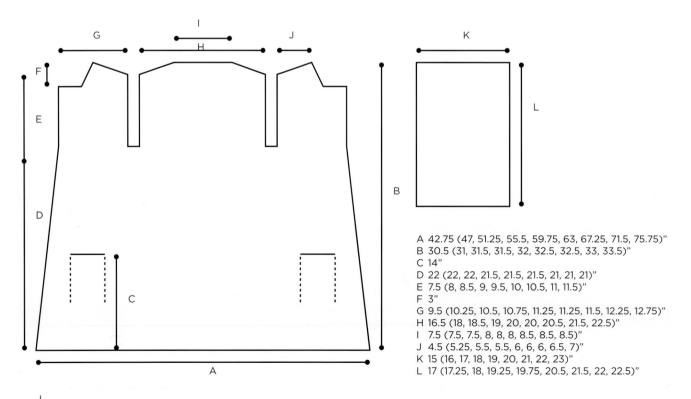

A 42.75 (47, 51.25, 55.5, 59.75, 63, 67.25, 71.5, 75.75)"
B 30.5 (31, 31.5, 31.5, 32, 32.5, 32.5, 33, 33.5)"
C 14"
D 22 (22, 22, 21.5, 21.5, 21.5, 21, 21, 21)"
E 7.5 (8, 8.5, 9, 9.5, 10, 10.5, 11, 11.5)"
F 3"
G 9.5 (10.25, 10.5, 10.75, 11.25, 11.25, 11.5, 12.25, 12.75)"
H 16.5 (18, 18.5, 19, 20, 20, 20.5, 21.5, 22.5)"
I 7.5 (7.5, 7.5, 8, 8, 8, 8.5, 8.5, 8.5)"
J 4.5 (5.25, 5.5, 5.5, 6, 6, 6, 6.5, 7)"
K 15 (16, 17, 18, 19, 20, 21, 22, 23)"
L 17 (17.25, 18, 19.25, 19.75, 20.5, 21.5, 22, 22.5)"

Abbreviations			and back of stitch	PU	pick up	SSP	sl, sl, p these 2 sts
BO	bind off	K-wise	knitwise	P-wise	purlwise		tog tbl
cn	cable needle	LH	left hand	rep	repeat	SSSK	sl, sl, sl, k these 3 sts
CC	contrast color	M	marker	Rev St st	reverse stockinette		tog
CDD	Centered double	M1	make one stitch		stitch	St st	stockinette stitch
	dec	M1L	make one left-lean-	RH	right hand	sts	stitch(es)
CO	cast on		ing stitch	rnd(s)	round(s)	TBL	through back loop
cont	continue	M1R	make one right-	RS	right side	TFL	through front loop
dec	decrease(es)		leaning stitch	Sk	skip	tog	together
DPN(s)	double pointed	MC	main color	Sk2p	sl 1, k2tog, pass	W&T	wrap & turn (see
	needle(s)	P	purl		slipped stitch over		specific instructions
EOR	every other row	P2tog	purl 2 sts together		k2tog: 2 sts dec		in pattern)
inc	increase	PM	place marker	SKP	sl, k, psso: 1 st dec	WE	work even
K	knit	PFB	purl into the front	SL	slip	WS	wrong side
K2tog	knit two sts to-		and back of stitch	SM	slip marker	WYIB	with yarn in back
	gether	PSSO	pass slipped stitch	SSK	sl, sl, k these 2 sts	WYIF	with yarn in front
KFB	knit into the front		over		tog	YO	yarn over

LUXE

by Tabetha Hedrick

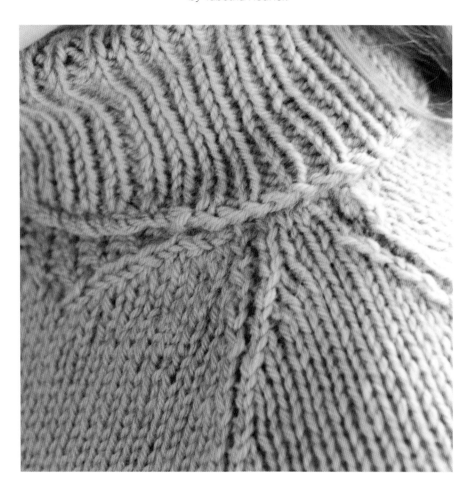

SIZES
XS (S, M, L, XL, 2XL, 3XL).

FINISHED MEASUREMENTS
32 (35 3/4, 37 3/4, 42 1/4, 46, 51 3/4, 53 3/4)" finished bust measurement; garment is meant to be worn with 1.75 - 2.25" of positive ease.

YARN
Knit Picks Wool of the Andes Worsted (100% Peruvian Highland Wool; 110 yards/50g):
Almond 25072, 8 (9, 10, 11, 13, 14, 15) balls.

NEEDLES
US 9 (5.5mm) knitting needles, or size to obtain gauge
US 9 (5.5mm) 16" circular knitting needles

NOTIONS
Tapestry Needle
Stitch marker

GAUGE
17 sts and 22 rows = 4" over in Stockinette Stitch, blocked.
19.5 sts and 26 rows = 4" in Twisted Rib, lightly stretched and blocked.

Luxe

Notes:

The first and last st of every St st row is knit to create a Garter selvedge edge for seaming.

Instructions are given for the smallest size with larger sizes in parentheses. When only one number is given, it applies to all sizes. When a '0' or '-' is used, no stitches are worked for that size.

Stitch Patterns

Twisted Rib (multiple of 2 sts + 2):
All Rows: K1, *k1tbl, p1; rep from * to last st, k1.

Stockinette Stitch (any number of sts):
Row 1 (RS): K.
Row 2: K1, p to last st, k1.

Collar (multiple of 2 sts):
All Rounds: *K1tbl, p1; rep to end.

DIRECTIONS

Back
CO 78 (82, 88, 96, 104, 116, 122) sts.
Work Twisted Rib patt for a total of 12 rows.
Change to St st and work 2 rows.

Shape Waist
Dec Row (RS): K1, ssk, k to last 3 sts, k2tog, k1 – 2 sts dec'd.

Continuing in St st, rep Dec Row every 10 (10, 14, 22, 12, 10, 12) rows 1 (1, 1, 1, 3, 5, 3) more time(s), then every 12 (12, 16, 24, 14, 0, 14) rows 2 (2, 1, 0, 0, 0, 0) time(s) – 70 (74, 82, 92, 96, 106, 114) sts.

Work evenly in St st until Back measures a finished length of 11.5 (11.5, 11.5, 11.5, 12.25, 12.25, 12.25)" from cast-on edge, ending with a WS row.

Sizes S, XL, 2XL, and 3XL ONLY:
Inc Row (RS): K1, M1, k to last st, M1, k1 – 2 sts inc'd.

Continuing in St st, rep Inc Row every ----- (6, ------, -------, 6, 4, 14) rows - (1, ------, ------, 1, 2, 0) more times.

All Sizes:
Work evenly in St st until Back measures 12.75 (12.75, 13.25, 13.5, 14.25, 14.25, 14.25)" from cast-on edge, ending with a WS row.

Shape Armhole
Bind off 2 (3, 3, 5, 6, 9, 10) sts at beg of each of next 2 rows – 66 (72, 76, 82, 88, 94, 96) sts rem.

Dec Row (RS): K1, ssk, work to last 3 sts, k2tog, k1 – 2 sts dec'd.

Continuing in St st, rep Dec Row every 4 (4, 2, 2, 2, 2, 2) rows 10 (14, 2, 4, 7, 12, 12) more times, then every 6 (0, 4, 4, 4, 4, 4) rows 2 (0, 13, 13, 12, 10, 11) times.

Work 5 (3, 3, 3, 3, 3, 3) rows evenly in St st, ending with a WS row.

Bind off rem 40, (42, 44, 46, 48, 48, 48) sts.

Front
Work as for Back to armhole.

Shape Armhole
Bind off 2 (3, 3, 5, 6, 9, 10) sts at beg of each of next 2 rows – 66 (72, 76, 82, 88, 94, 96) sts rem.

Note: Front Neck Shaping begins shortly after Armhole Shaping and is worked at the same time, so read the next section carefully.

Dec Row (RS): K1, ssk, work in St st to last 3 sts, k2tog, k1 – 2 sts dec'd.

Repeat Dec Row every 4 (4, 2, 2, 2, 2, 2) rows 10 (14, 2, 4, 7, 12, 12) more times, then every 6 (0, 4, 4, 4, 4, 4) rows 2 (0, 13, 13, 12, 10, 11) times.

Work 5 (3, 3, 3, 3, 3, 3) rows evenly in St st, ending with a WS row.

AT THE SAME TIME, when armhole measures a finished length of 7.5 (8, 7.75, 8, 8, 8, 8.75)", begin Front Neck Shaping on the next RS row as follows:

Shape Front Neck
Next Row (RS): Bind off center 18 (20, 20, 22, 22, 22, 22) sts.
Next Row (WS): Work in St st, joining a new ball of yarn on the opposite side of neck.

Note: Both sides of the neck are worked at the same time.

Dec Row 1 (RS): Work in St st to 3 sts before neck edge, k2tog, k1, move to other side of neck, k1, ssk, knit to end - 1 st dec'd each side of neck.

Working in St st, rep Dec Row 1 every RS row 4 (4, 5, 7, 8, 10, 10) more times.

Sizes XS, S, M, L, and XL ONLY:
Dec Row 2 (RS): Work in St st to 4 sts before neck edge, k3tog, k1, move to other side of neck, k1, s2kp, knit to end - 2 sts dec'd each side of neck.

Working in St st, rep Dec Row 2 every RS row 1 (1, 1, 0, 0, -, -) more time.

All Sizes:
When all Armhole and Neck Shaping is complete, 2 sts rem on each side of the neck. Bind off those 2 sts on next RS row.

Sleeves
CO 50 (52, 54, 58, 62, 64, 66) sts.
Work Twisted Rib patt for a total of 14 rows.
Change to St st and work even for 2 rows.

Shape Sleeve
Inc Row (RS): K1, M1, work in St st to last st, M1, k1 – 2 sts inc'd.

Working in St st, rep Inc Row every 8 (8, 6, 6, 6, 4, 2) rows 1 (1, 1, 1, 3, 7, 4) more times, then every 10 (10, 8, 8, 8, 6, 4) rows 1 (1, 2, 2, 1, 0, 6) times - 56 (58, 62, 66, 72, 80, 88) sts.

Work evenly in St st until Sleeve measures 9.5 (9.5, 10.25, 10.25, 10.5, 10.5, 11)" from cast-on edge, ending with a WS row.

Shape Cap
Bind off 2 (3, 3, 5, 6, 9, 10) sts at beg of each of next 2 rows - 52

(52, 56, 56, 60, 62, 68) sts rem.

Dec Row (RS): K1, ssk, k to last 3 sts, k2tog, k1 – 2 sts dec'd.

Working in St st, rep Dec Row every RS row 17 (16, 17, 16, 17, 18, 20) more times, then every 4 rows 5 (6, 6, 7, 7, 7, 7) times.

Work 3 rows evenly in St st, ending with a WS row.

Bind off rem 6 (6, 8, 8, 10, 10, 12) sts on next RS row.

Pockets (make 2)
CO 17 sts. Work Twisted Rib patt for 26 rows. Bind off loosely.

Finishing
Weave in ends, wash and block to diagram. With yarn threaded on a tapestry needle, sleeve caps to raglan armholes. Sew side and sleeve seams.

Pockets
Pin pockets approx. 1" from hem ribbing and 3" from side seams. Sew in place.

Abbreviations		rem	Remaining
CO	Cast Off	rep	Repeat
dec	Decrease(d)	RS	Right Side
inc	Increase(d)	S2kp	Slip next stitch as
K	Knit		if to knit, k2tog,
Ktbl	Knit through the		pass slipped stitch
	back loop		over. 2 sts dec.
K2tog	Knit 2 together	SSK	Slip, Slip, Knit
K3tog	Knit 3 together	St st	Stockinette stitch
M1	Make 1	WS	Wrong Side
P	Purl		

Collar
With circular needle and beginning at left front neck edge with RS facing, pick up and knit 11 (11, 12, 14, 15, 17, 17) sts from left front neck edge, 18 (20, 20, 22, 22, 22, 22) sts from center front neck bind-off sts, 11 (11, 12, 14, 15, 17, 17) sts from right front neck edge, and 40 (42, 44, 46, 48, 48, 48) sts from back neck bind-off sts - 80 (84, 88, 96, 100, 104, 104). Place marker and join to work in the round. Work Collar patt until collar measures 7" from neck edge or to desired length. Bind off all sts loosely.

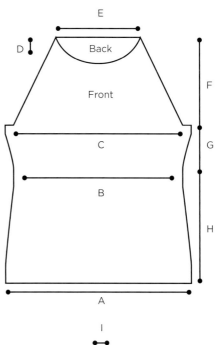

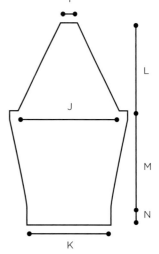

A 18.25 (19.25, 20.75, 22.5, 24.5, 27.25, 28.75)"
B 16.5 (17.5, 19.25, 21.75, 22.5, 25, 26.75)"
C 16.5 (18.25, 19.25, 21.75, 23.5, 26.25, 27.25)"
D 3 (3, 3.25, 3.25, 4, 4.25, 4.25)"
E 8.5 (9, 9.5, 10, 10.25, 10.25, 10.25)"
F 10.5 (11, 11, 11.75, 12, 12.25, 13)"
G 3.25 (3.25, 3.75, 4.75, 4.5, 4.75, 5.5)"
H 11.5 (11.5, 11.5, 11.5, 12.25, 12.25, 12.25)"
I 1.5 (1.5, 2, 2, 2.25, 2.25, 2.75)"
J 13.25 (13.75, 14.5, 15.5, 17, 18.75, 20.75)"
K 11.75 (12.25, 12.75, 13.75, 14.5, 15, 15.5)"
L 10.5 (11, 11, 11.75, 12, 12.25, 13)"
M 7.25 (7.25, 7.75, 7.75, 8.25, 8.25, 8.75)"
N 2.25"

Knit Picks yarn is both luxe and affordable—a seeming contradiction trounced! But it's not just about the pretty colors; we also care deeply about fiber quality and fair labor practices, leaving you with a gorgeously reliable product you'll turn to time and time again.

This collection features

Wool of the Andes
Bulky Weight
100% Peruvian Highland Wool

Capra
DK Weight
85% Merino wool, 15% Cashmere

Wool of the Andes
Worsted Weight
100% Peruvian Highland Wool

City Tweed
Aran Weight
55% Merino Wool, 25% Superfine Alpaca, 20% Donegal Tweed

Capretta
Fingering Weight
80% Merino wool, 10% Cashmere, 10% Nylon

Gloss
DK Weight
70% Merino Wool, 30% Silk

City Tweed
DK Weight
55% Merino Wool, 25% Superfine Alpaca, 20% Donegal Tweed

View these beautiful yarns and more at www.KnitPicks.com

Swish Bulky
Bulky Weight
100% Superwash Merino Wool